FIGMA USER GUIDE

The Comprehensive Handbook to Understand this Web-Based Interface Design Tool

BURT P. SOUZA

Copyright © 2024 Burt P. Souza
All Rights Reserved

No part of this publication may be reproduced, distributed, or transmitted in any form or by any means, including photocopying, recording, or other electronic or mechanical methods, without the prior written permission of the publisher, except in the case of brief quotations embodied in critical reviews and certain other non-commercial uses permitted by copyright law

DISCLAIMER

The contents of this book are provided for informational and entertainment purposes only. The author and publisher make no representations or warranties with respect to the accuracy, applicability, completeness, or suitability of the contents of this book for any purpose.

The information contained within this book is based on the author's personal experiences, research, and opinions, and it is not intended to substitute for professional advice. Readers are encouraged to consult appropriate professionals in the field regarding their individual situations and circumstances.

The author and publisher shall not be liable for any loss, injury, or damage allegedly arising from any information or suggestions contained within this book. Any reliance you place on such information is strictly at your own risk.

Furthermore, the inclusion of any third-party resources, websites, or references does not imply endorsement or responsibility for the content or services provided by these entities.

Readers are encouraged to use their own discretion and judgment in applying any information or recommendations contained within this book to their own lives and situations.

All rights reserved. No part of this book may be reproduced, distributed, or transmitted in any form or by any means, including photocopying, recording, or other electronic or mechanical methods, without the prior written permission of the publisher, except in the case of brief quotations embodied in critical reviews and certain other non-commercial uses permitted by copyright law.

Thank you for reading and understanding this disclaimer

TABLE OF CONTENTS

DISCLAIMER 2
CHAPTER ONE 6
   INTRODUCTION TO FIGMA 6
   What is Figma? 6
   Key Features and Benefits of Figma 7
   Figma Interface 10
CHAPTER TWO 12
   GETTING STARTED WITH FIGMA 12
   Signing Up and Setting Up Your Workspace 12
   Understanding Figma Files, Projects and Teams 16
   Importing and Exporting Designs in Figma 20
CHAPTER THREE 24
   DESIGN ESSENTIALS IN FIGMA 24
   Working with Frames and Logos 24
   Using Vector Tools and Design Elements 31
   Text Styles, Topography and Text Editing 35
   Creating and Applying Colors, Fills and Effects 38
CHAPTER FOUR 42
   DESIGN SYSTEMS AND STYLE GUIDES 42
   Establishing a Design System for Consistency 42
   Creating and Managing Styles 43
   Using Libraries and Components for Reusability 46
CHAPTER FIVE 52
   BUILDING USER INTERFACE ELEMENTS 52
   Designing Buttons, Icons and Input Fields 52
   Creating Navigating Bars, Menus and Dropdowns 55
   Creating Variants for Different Design States 57

    Designing Interactive Elements and Microinteractions 60

CHAPTER SIX 62

ADVANCED DESIGN TECHNIQUES IN FIGMA 62

Grids, Layouts and Auto Layout for Responsive Design 62

Using Constraints and Resizing for Design Flexibility 65

Creating Variants for Different Design States 68

Design for Accessibility in Figma 69

CHAPTER SEVEN 72

PROTOTYPING BASICS AND TECHNIQUES 72

Introduction to Prototyping in Figma 72

Connecting Frames and Creating User Flows 73

Previewing and Sharing Prototypes 79

CHAPTER EIGHT 84

USER TESTING AND COLLABORATION 84

Planning and Conducting User Testing Sessions 84

Using Figma for User Feedback and Iteration 87

Collaboration Tools and Features in Figma 89

CHAPTER NINE 92

PLUGINS AND INTEGRATION TO ENHANCE FIGMA 92

Exploring Figma Plugin Ecosystem 92

Using Plugin to Supercharge Your Design Workflow 96

Integrating Figma with Other Design and Development Tools 97

CHAPTER TEN 100

DESIGN HANDOFF AND DEVELOPMENT 100

Preparing Design Assets for Developers 100

Using Figma for Developer Specifications and Style Guides 102

Collaboration Between Designers and Developers 103

CHAPTER ELEVEN 106

ADVANCED CUSTOMIZATION AND WORKFLOWS 106

- Customizing Your Figma Workspace 106
- Keyboard Shortcuts 107
- Advanced Tips and Tricks for Expert Figma Users 110

CHAPTER TWELVE 114
TROUBLESHOOTING AND RESOURCES 114
- Common Issues and Solutions 114

CHAPTER THIRTEEN 120
APPENDIX 120
- Glossary of Figma Terms 120

CHAPTER ONE
INTRODUCTION TO FIGMA

What is Figma?

Figma is an advanced, browser-based tool specifically crafted for collaborative user interface (UI) design. Launched in 2016, it has rapidly gained popularity within the web design industry and among online communities. Unlike traditional design tools, Figma enables multiple users to collaborate simultaneously in real-time, fostering seamless teamwork on vibrant and interactive prototypes.

At its core, Figma harnesses the power of vector graphics to empower design teams. They can create intricate wireframes and layouts that adapt fluidly to different screen sizes, ensuring a responsive and user-friendly experience across devices. Designers can add dynamic elements such as scrolling effects and interactive hover states, ensuring that prototypes not only look polished but also function realistically.

One of Figma's standout features is its capability to facilitate rapid prototyping and iteration. Design teams can quickly build and test functional UIs and web applications. Moreover, Figma streamlines the transition from design to development by allowing designers to export code snippets directly from their prototypes. This feature supports a smoother handoff process, ensuring that developers can implement designs accurately and efficiently.

Beyond its technical capabilities, Figma boasts a robust community ecosystem. This community actively contributes to the platform by developing plugins, sharing templates, and refining widgets. Through Figma's dedicated platform and other collaborative forums, designers can exchange ideas, receive feedback, and improve their designs collaboratively. This community-driven approach not only enhances the tool's functionality but also encourages innovation and creativity in UI and web design.

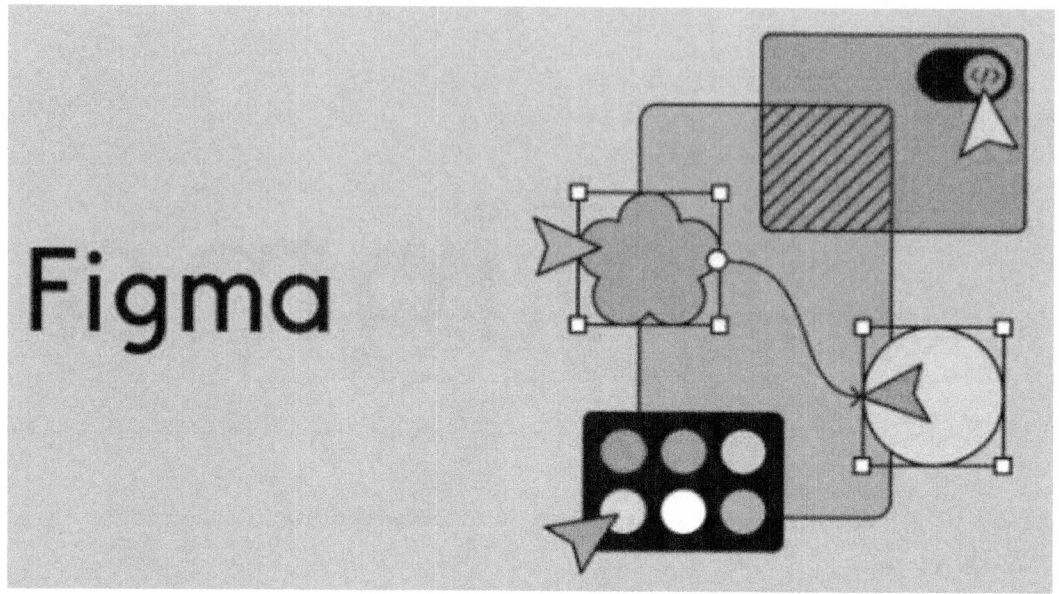

Ultimately, Figma transcends traditional design software by fostering a global network of designers and developers. It empowers teams not only to collaborate internally but also to tap into a vast pool of collective knowledge and expertise. This communal spirit not only accelerates the design process but also ensures that users can continuously refine and elevate their design standards in a collaborative and supportive environment."

Key Features and Benefits of Figma
Key Features:

Real-time Collaboration: Figma enables multiple users to collaborate simultaneously on the same design project, ensuring seamless and efficient teamwork.

Browser-Based Platform: Operating directly in a web browser, Figma eliminates the need for software installation, enabling access to projects from any internet-connected device.

Vector Graphics Editing: It offers robust tools for editing vector graphics, allowing designers to create scalable, high-quality designs suitable for various screen sizes and resolutions.

Interactive Prototyping: Designers can create interactive prototypes with animations, transitions, and gestures directly within Figma, enhancing realism in user experiences during the design phase.

Component-Based Design System: Figma supports reusable components and styles, enabling designers to maintain consistency across multiple projects efficiently.

Version History and Comments: It includes features for tracking version history and leaving comments, facilitating collaborative iteration and feedback on designs.

Design Handoff and Collaboration with Developers: Figma simplifies the handoff process by enabling designers to generate design specifications and export assets directly for developers, ensuring accurate implementation.

Plugins and Integrations: The platform supports a diverse array of plugins and integrations, extending its functionality and enabling users to customize workflows and integrate seamlessly with other tools.

Community and Resources: Figma hosts a dynamic community where designers can share resources, templates, and plugins, fostering collaboration, knowledge exchange, and continuous learning.

Benefits:

Efficient Collaboration: Teams collaborate more effectively, reducing iteration cycles and enhancing productivity.

Accessibility and Flexibility: As a browser-based tool, Figma offers accessibility across devices, facilitating convenient remote work and collaboration.

Scalability: Its vector-based approach ensures designs maintain clarity and scalability across various devices and screen sizes.

Consistent Design: Use of components and styles promotes consistency across projects, saving time and reinforcing brand identity.

User-Centric Prototyping: Interactive prototypes validate design concepts early, ensuring final products meet user expectations and requirements.

Developer Collaboration: Seamless design-to-development handoff streamlines workflows and minimizes errors during implementation.

Innovation via Plugins: Access to plugins and community-driven resources enhances functionality and inspires innovation in design processes.

These features and benefits collectively position Figma as a robust tool for modern UI/UX design, fostering creativity, collaboration, and efficiency in design workflows.

Figma Interface

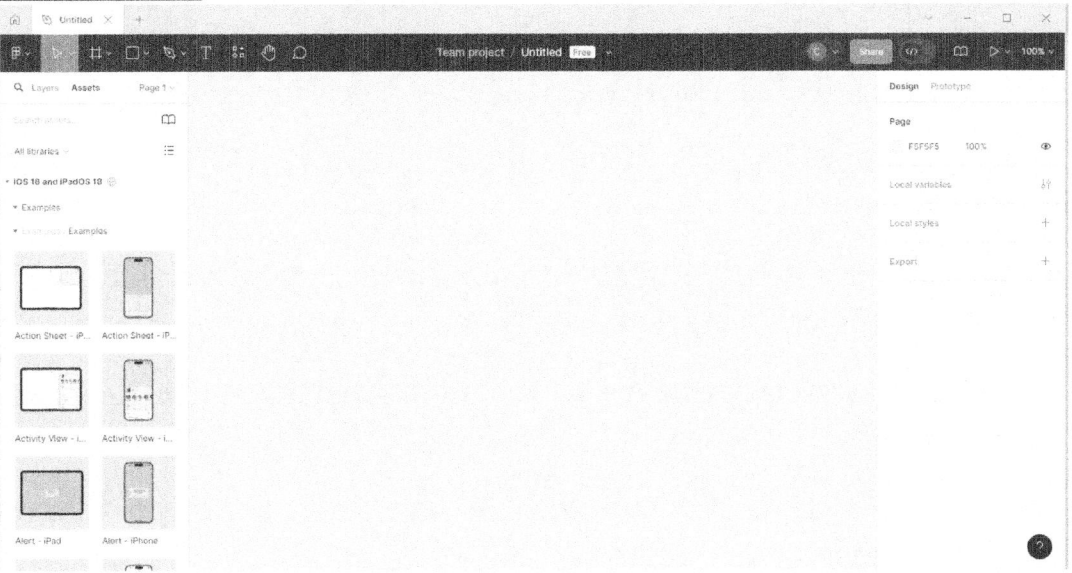

Figma's interface is crafted to enhance design workflows seamlessly. Here's an overview of its key components:

Canvas:

- This central workspace is where designs are created. Frames, representing screens or artboards, can be added and various tools used to build the UI.

Toolbar:

- Situated at the top, the toolbar offers quick access to essential tools for adding shapes, text, lines, and other design elements.

Layers Panel:

- Found on the left side, the layers panel lists all elements on the canvas. It enables organizing, editing, and managing visibility of layers for easier control.

Properties Panel:

- Located on the right side, the properties panel presents options for adjusting attributes like size, color, typography, and effects of the selected element.

Asset Panel (Optional):

- Optionally available as a plugin, this panel manages reusable components, styles, and colors within the project to ensure design consistency.

Navigation Bar:

- Positioned at the top, the navigation bar provides access to file management, project settings, collaboration tools (like inviting team members), and account settings.

Additional Features:

- Search: Quickly locate specific design elements, styles, or assets within the project for efficient navigation.

- Version History: Track changes in design files and revert to earlier versions if necessary.

- Prototyping Mode: Link frames to create interactive prototypes that simulate user interactions and workflows.

In summary, Figma's interface is clean, intuitive, and prioritizes easy access to design tools, maintaining focus on the creative process.

CHAPTER TWO
GETTING STARTED WITH FIGMA

Signing Up and Setting Up Your Workspace
Sign Up for Figma with Email and Password:

- Go to Figma.com and click on "Sign up" or "Log in" in the top right corner.

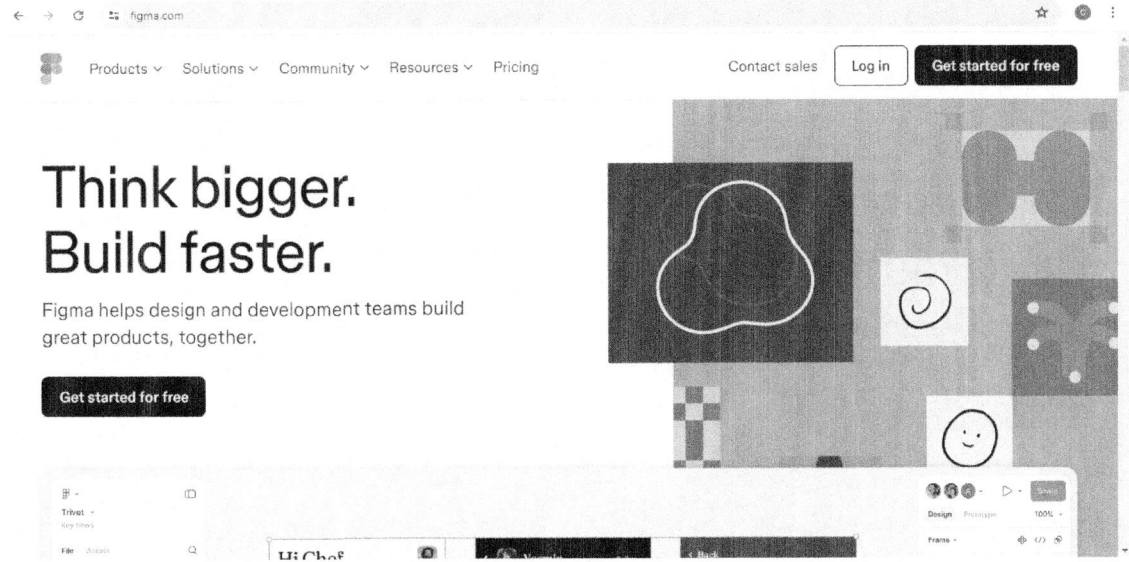

- Enter your email address in the provided field.

- Create and enter a unique password in the field below.

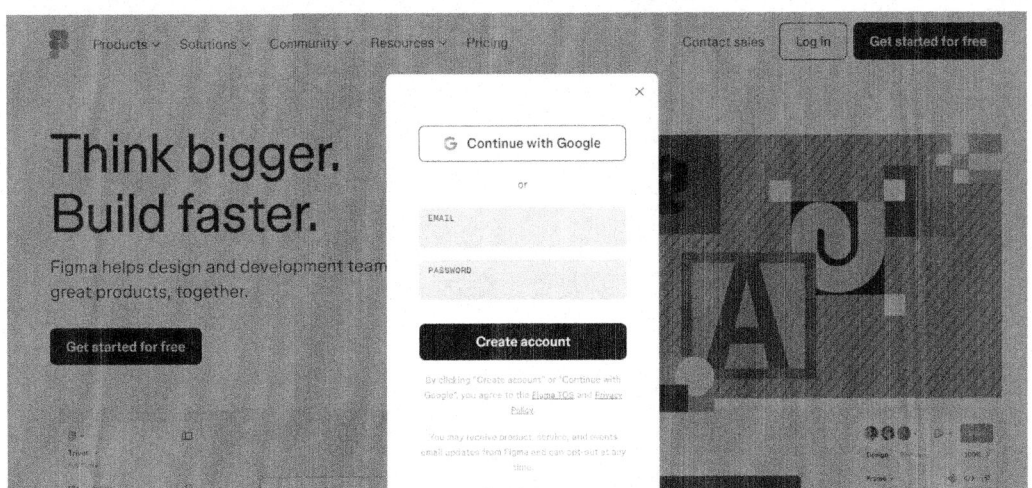

- Click the "Sign up" button to complete the registration. You will be automatically logged into your new Figma account.

- Check your email for a verification message from Figma. Click the verification link to finalize the setup and access your new account.

Sign Up with a Google Account:

- Visit Figma.com and click "Sign up" or "Log in" in the top right corner, or use this link directly: https://www.figma.com/signup.

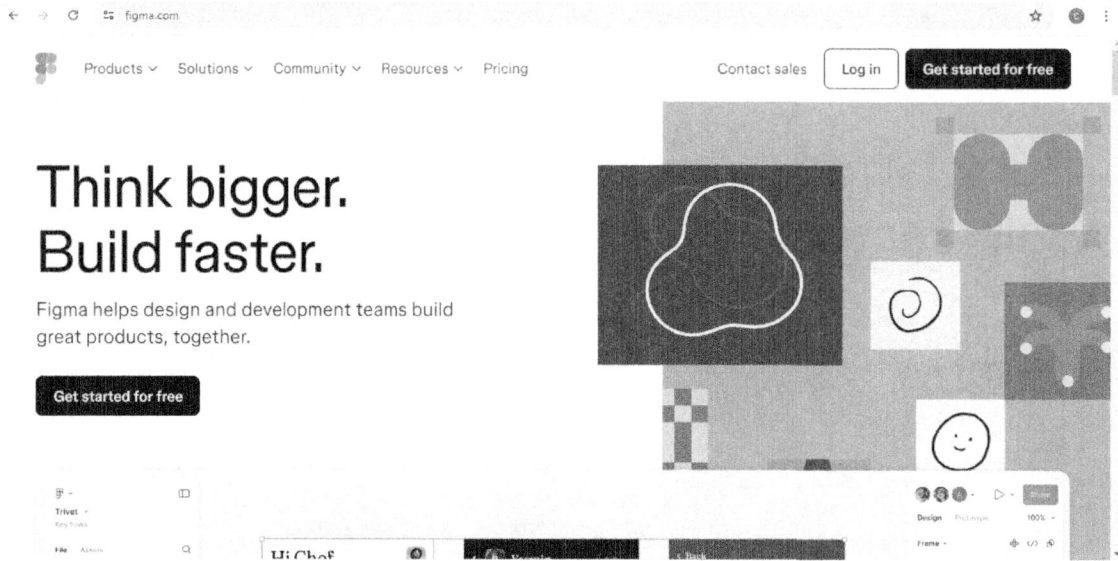

- Select "Continue with Google" at the top of the window.

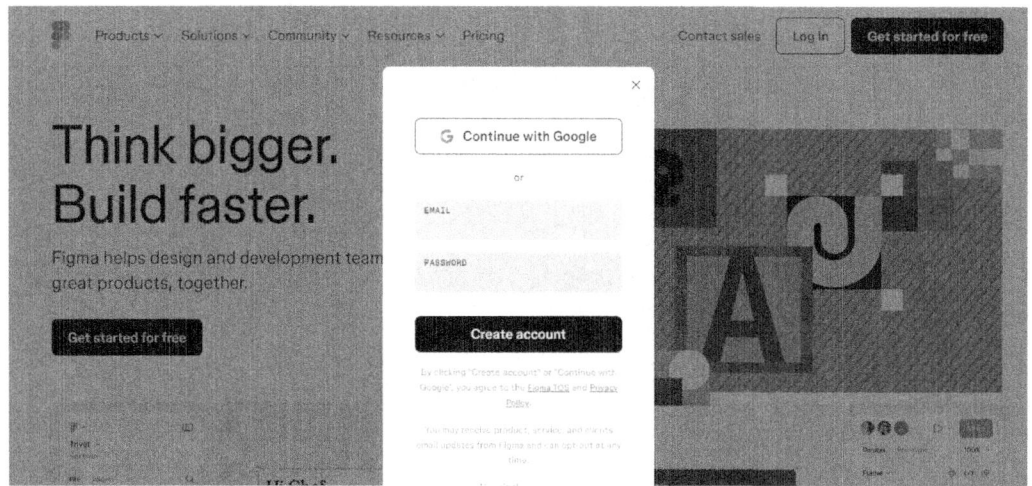

- If you're already logged into Google, confirm your details. If not, enter your Google email or phone number and click "Next."

13

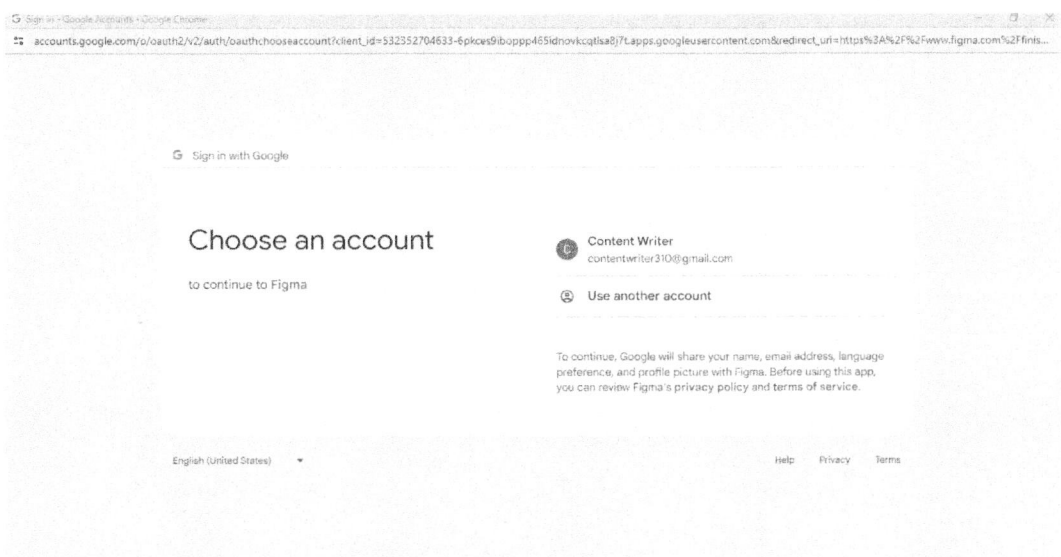

- Enter your Google password and click "Next" to finish. A Figma account will be created with your Google credentials.
- After signing up, Figma directs you to the file browser, where you can access your unlimited Drafts folder, any teams you are part of, and the Figma Community.

Creating Teams:

- To collaborate with other designers, you can create teams in Figma.

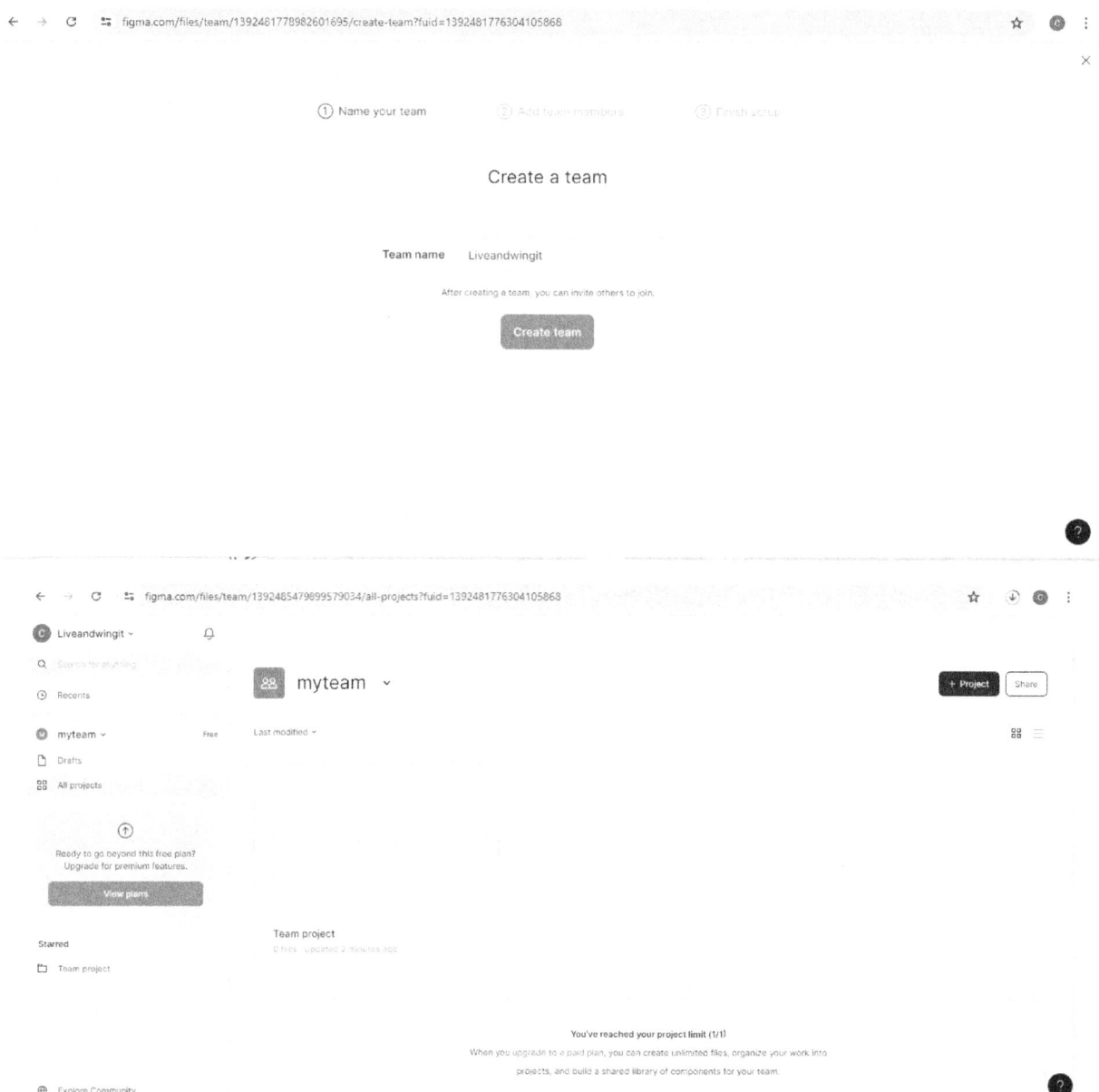

Setting Up a Workspace:

Workspaces are collections of teams, people, and resources within an organization. They can be created for different groups, departments, or business units.

Steps to Set Up a Workspace:

Create a New Workspace:

- Select "Admin" from the left sidebar.
- Click "Workspaces" in the menu bar.

- Click "New workspace" at the top of the table.
- Name the workspace and add at least one workspace admin by typing an existing member's name and selecting it.
- Click "Create workspace" to complete the process.

Assign Teams to the Workspace:

- Workspace admins can manage teams within the workspace.

Assign Members and Guests (Optional):

- Organization admins can assign members to any workspace, while workspace admins can only assign unassigned members to their managed workspaces. Members can join teams and access resources in other workspaces even if they are assigned to one workspace.

Additional Tips:

- Hidden Workspaces: You can make a workspace hidden in the "All workspaces" view for non-members.
- Default Teams: Workspace admins can set default teams for members, automatically adding them to these teams.
- Self-Assignment: Members can assign themselves to workspaces, simplifying the management process.

These steps and tips help streamline collaboration and organization within Figma, making it easier to manage teams and projects effectively.

Understanding Figma Files, Projects and Teams
Figma Files:

Figma files are the primary units where design activities take place. Each file can include multiple pages, frames, and design elements, enabling thorough project organization within a single document.

- Pages: Pages within a Figma file help segregate different sections or phases of a project. For instance, you might have distinct pages for wireframes, mockups, and final designs.

- Frames: Similar to artboards in other design tools, frames define specific areas of your design, representing screens or components within a project. Frames can be nested for complex layouts.

- Elements: These are the basic design components like shapes, text, images, and vectors that constitute the content of a frame.

Figma Projects:

Projects in Figma act as containers to organize related design files. They help keep work organized, particularly when managing multiple files for a single project or client.

- Creating a Project: From the Figma dashboard, select "New Project." Provide a name for your project and optionally add a description.

- Managing Files: Within a project, you can create, store, and manage multiple Figma files, grouping all related design work in one place.

- Permissions: Projects enable you to manage permissions, allowing control over who can view or edit the files within the project.

Figma Teams:

Teams in Figma are groups of users collaborating on projects. They offer a shared workspace where members can access projects, files, and resources.

- Creating a Team: On the Figma dashboard, select "New Team," enter a team name, and invite members via email.

- Team Projects: After creating a team, you can set up team projects within the shared workspace. All team members will have access based on their roles and permissions.

- Roles and Permissions: Figma allows assignment of roles such as Viewer, Editor, and Admin to team members, determining their actions within team projects.

Using Figma in Teams and Projects:

Organize Your Work:

- Use projects to group related files, simplifying the management and navigation of your design work.

- Use pages within files to separate different stages or aspects of your project.

Collaborate Efficiently:

- Invite team members to collaborate on projects, assigning roles based on their required access level.

- Utilize real-time collaboration and commenting to streamline the design process and gather feedback.

Manage Permissions:

- Control access to projects and files by setting appropriate permissions for team members.

- Use the admin role to manage team settings and members effectively.

By understanding and utilizing Figma's structure of files, projects, and teams, you can efficiently organize your design work, foster collaboration, and maintain control over the design process.

Importing and Exporting Designs in Figma

Figma bridges the gap between your existing design resources and future creations. Let's explore how to import and export designs seamlessly:

Importing Existing Work:

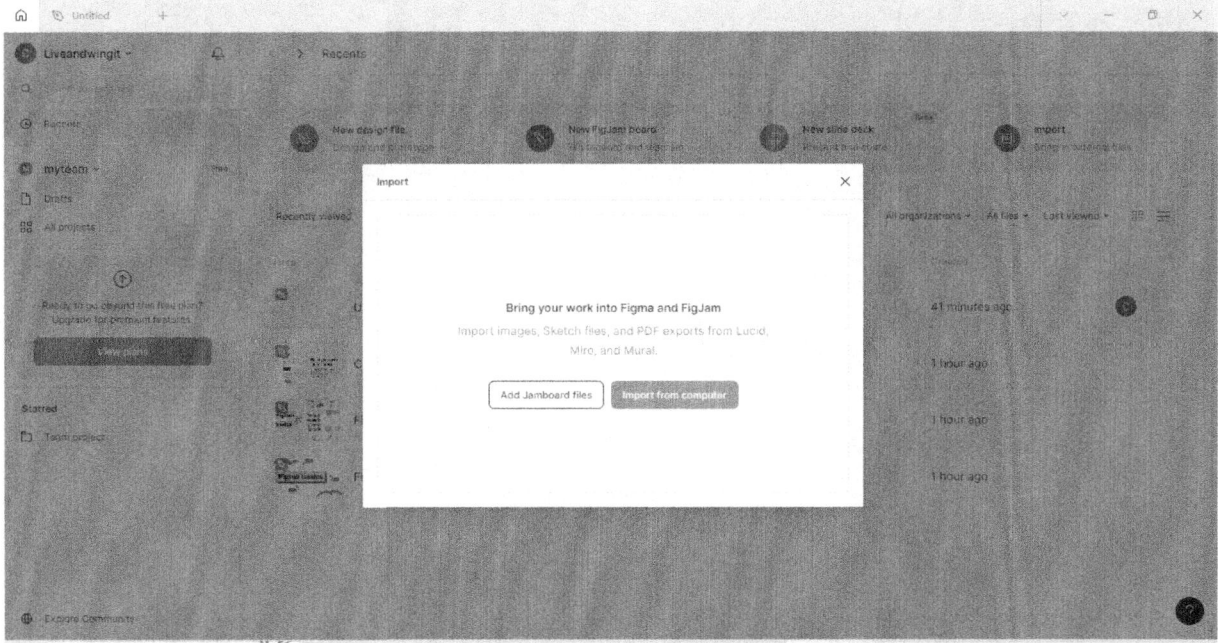

- Supported Formats: Breathe new life into old projects! Figma imports Sketch files (sketch), common image formats (PNG, JPG, GIF), and scalable vector graphics (SVGs).

- Importing Sketch Files: Effortlessly bring your Sketch projects into Figma. Just navigate to the file browser, click "Import," or drag and drop the Sketch file. Figma will convert it, preserving layers and elements.

- Images and SVGs: Importing images and SVGs is a breeze. Drag and drop them directly onto the canvas or use the "Place Image" option from the toolbar. You can even copy and paste elements from other design tools, and Figma will do its best to maintain formatting.

Sharing Your Designs:

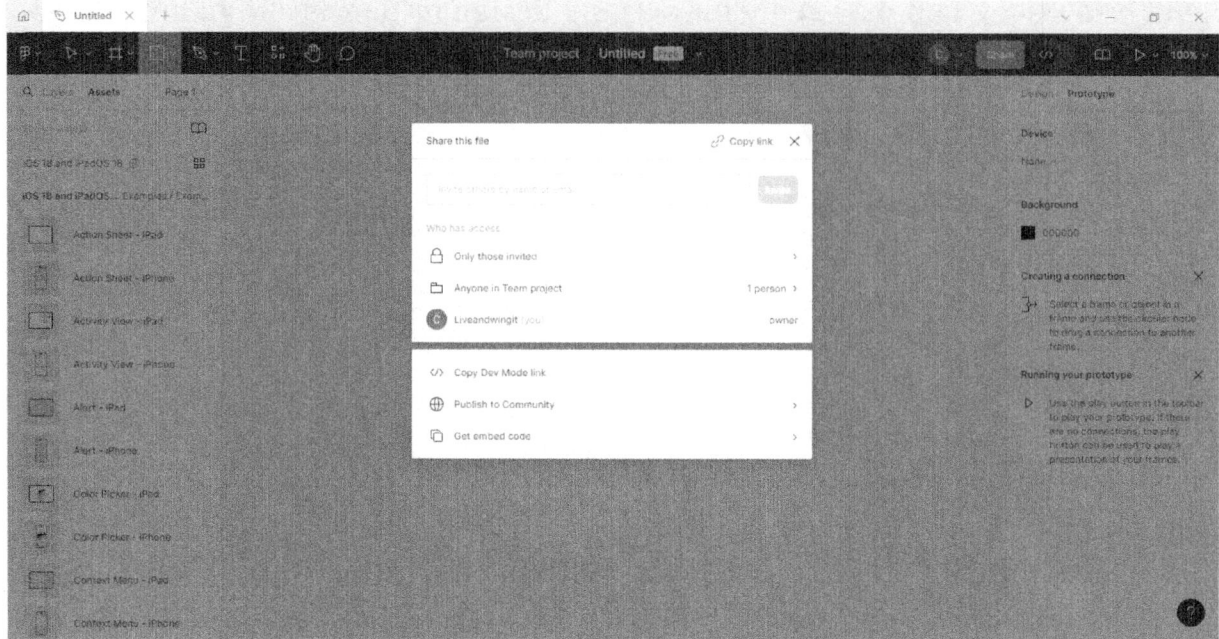

- Exporting Options: Tailor your exports to your needs. Choose from PNG, JPG, SVG, or PDF formats, and export entire frames, specific layers, or individual elements.

- Exporting the Essentials: Select the element(s) you want to export and head to the properties panel on the right. Click the "+" symbol under the "Export" section to choose the format and scale (e.g., 1x for regular size, 2x for double resolution).

- Batch Exporting: Need to export multiple items? Hold "Shift" while selecting layers or frames, then configure export settings for each. Click "Export" to process them all at once.

- Developer Friendly Exports: Figma caters to developers by offering CSS properties for design elements. Select an element and go to the "Code" tab in the properties panel to view and copy the code.

- Exporting Entire Pages: To export a whole page, select all its elements and set the export settings for the entire selection.

Additional Export Features:

- Batch exporting saves time for large projects.
- Export presets ensure consistency across projects with pre-configured settings.
- Third-party integrations with tools like Zeplin and Avocode streamline the handover process to developers.

By mastering Figma's import and export features, you can effortlessly combine existing design assets with your creative vision, and share your work effectively with anyone involved in the process.

CHAPTER THREE
DESIGN ESSENTIALS IN FIGMA

Working with Frames and Logos

Frames in Figma function similarly to artboards in other design software. They define distinct sections of your design, such as different screens, components, or project segments. Here's a comprehensive guide on using frames:

Creating Frames:

Using the Frame Tool:

Accessing the Tool:

- Select the "Frame" tool from the toolbar or press the "F" key.

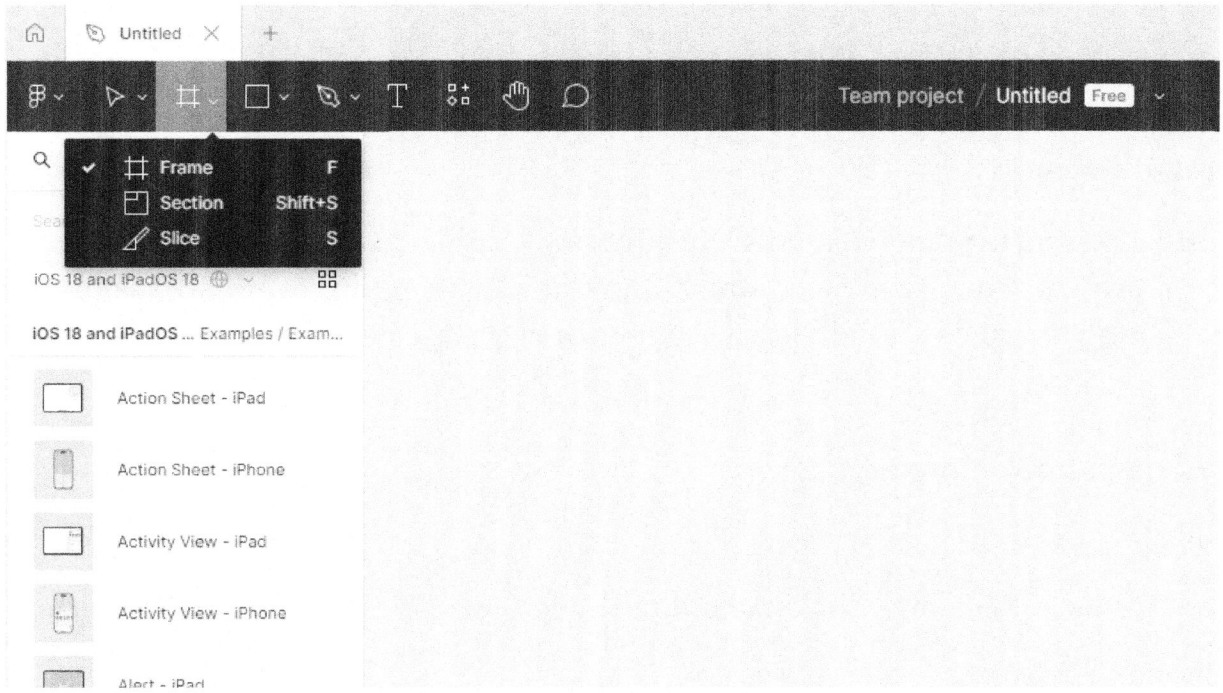

Creating a Frame:

- Click and drag on the canvas to draw a frame to your desired size.
- Alternatively, choose a preset frame size from the properties panel, like iPhone or Desktop.

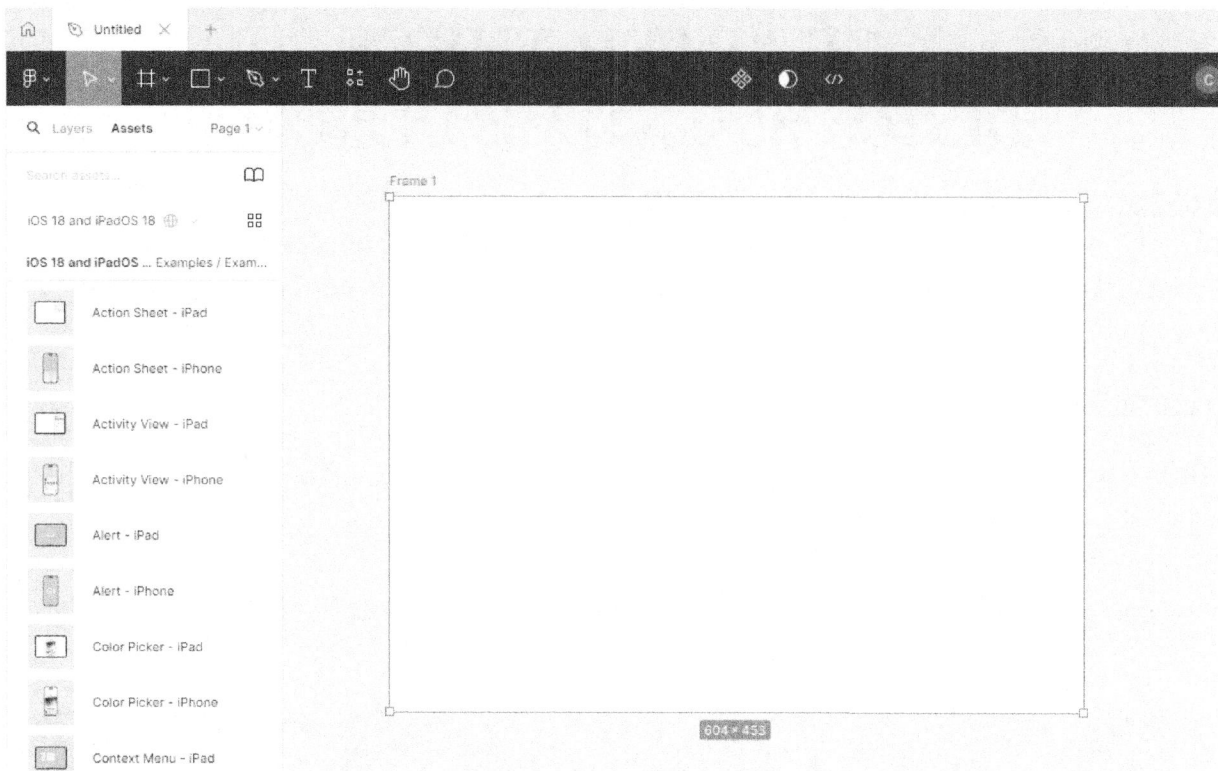

Nested Frames:

- Creating Complex Layouts: Nest frames within other frames to build intricate layouts. For instance, a parent frame might represent a full webpage, with nested frames for individual sections or components.

Resizing and Positioning:

Adjusting Size:

- Manual Resizing: Click and drag the edges or corners of a frame to resize.

Aligning Frames:

- Using Alignment Tools: Utilize the alignment tools in the toolbar to position frames precisely on the canvas.

Organizing Frames:

Naming Frames:

- Descriptive Labels: Name your frames clearly to keep your project organized, especially with multiple frames.

Grouping Frames:

- Combining Frames: Select related frames and press "Ctrl+G" (or "Cmd+G" on Mac) to group them. This helps manage complex designs with many frames.

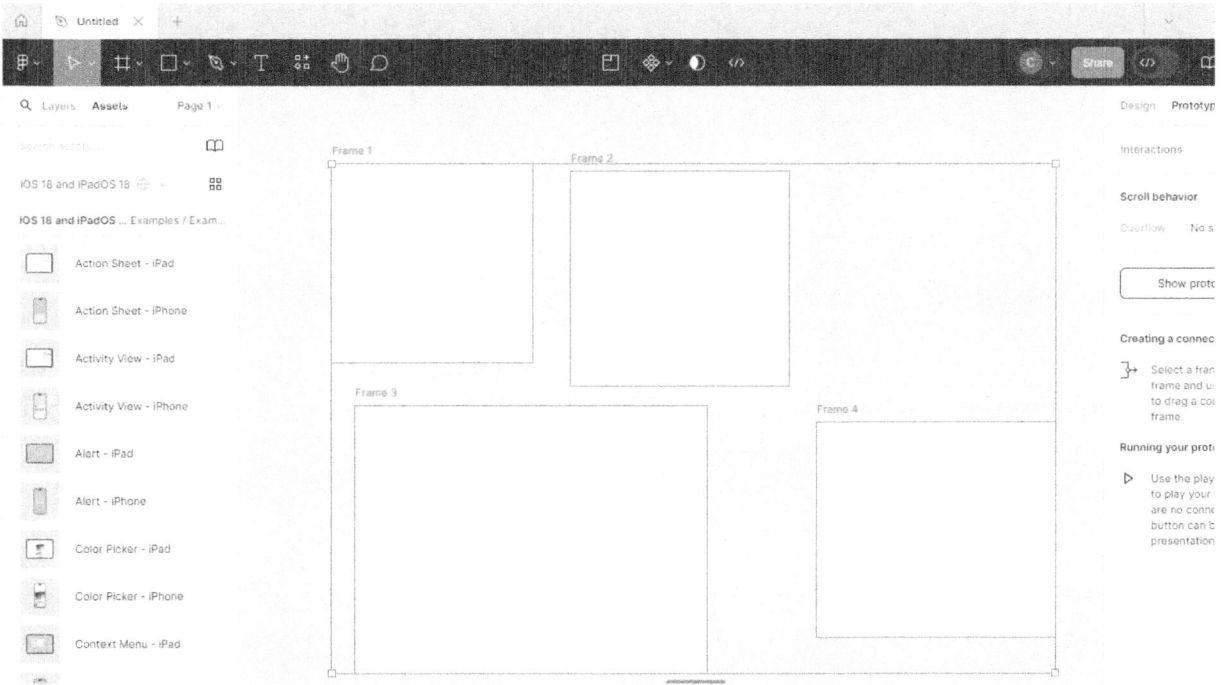

Using Pages:

- Segmenting Work: Use different pages within a Figma file to organize various phases or parts of your project.

Designing Within Frames:

Adding Elements:

- Shapes, Text, and Images: Incorporate shapes, text, images, and other design elements within frames. These can be moved, resized, and styled independently.

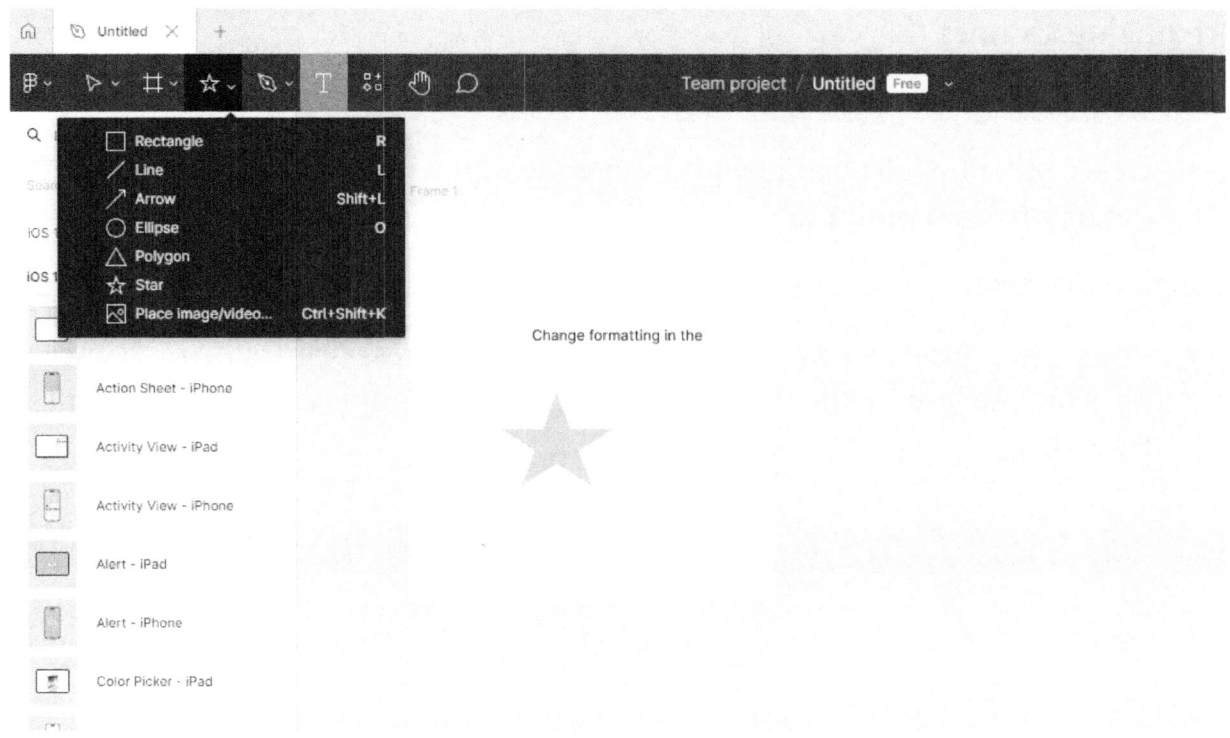

Applying Constraints:

- Responsive Design: Set constraints for elements within a frame to ensure they resize and reposition correctly when the frame changes size. For example, pin an element to the top-right corner of a frame.

Using Layout Grids:

- Maintaining Consistency: Apply layout grids to frames for design guidance. Choose from columns, rows, or grid layouts to ensure alignment and consistency.

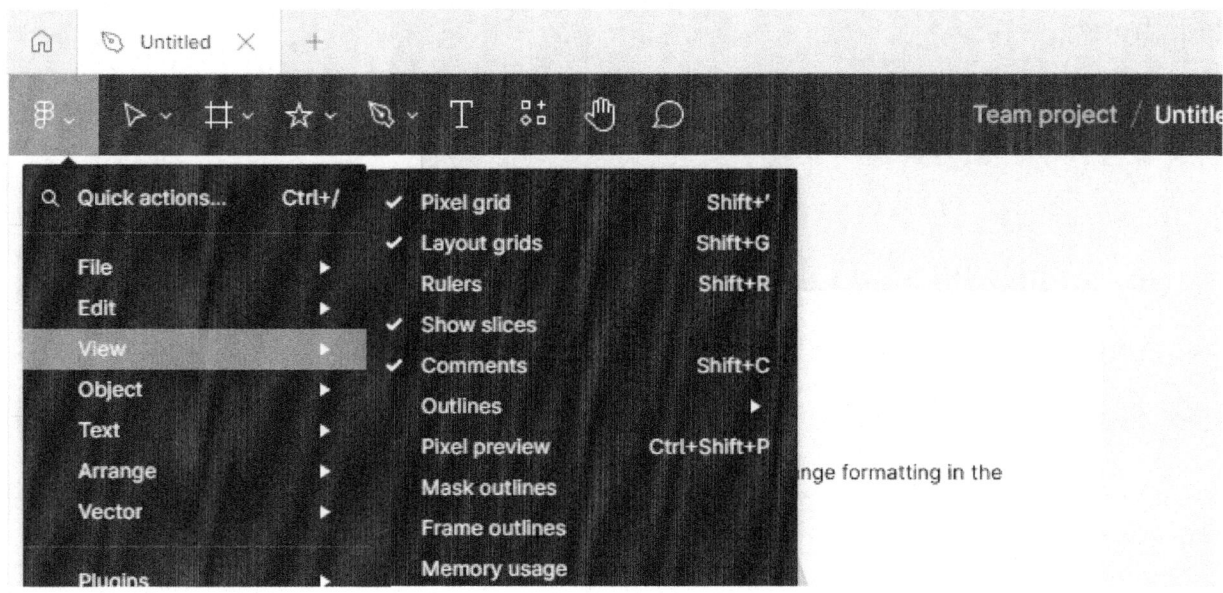

Working with Logos:

Logos are vital for brand representation. Here's how to handle logos effectively in Figma:

Importing Logos:

Drag and Drop:

- Direct Import: Drag and drop a logo file (PNG, JPG, SVG) from your computer directly onto the Figma canvas.

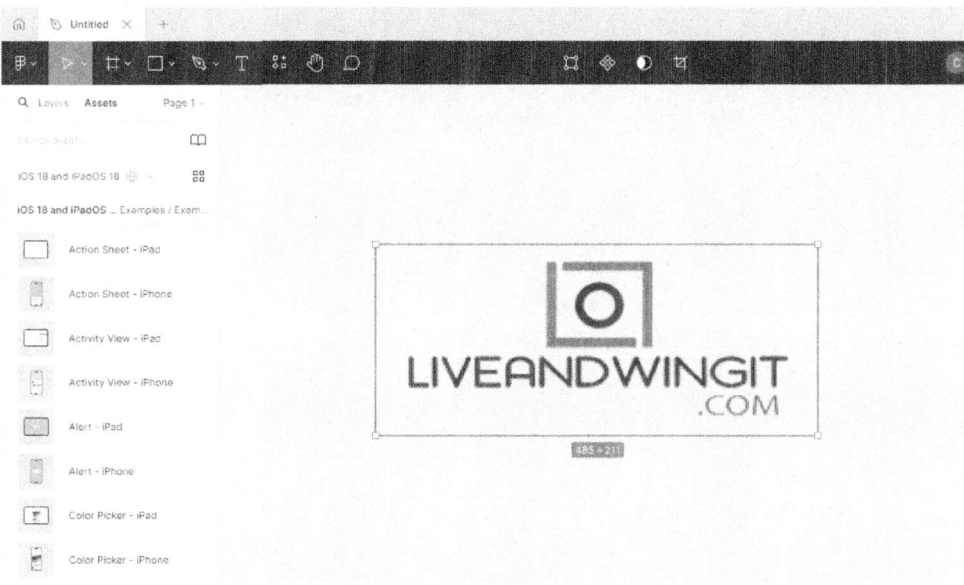

Place Image Tool:

- Selecting Files: Use the "Place Image" tool from the toolbar to select and position logo files on the canvas.

Resizing and Positioning Logos:

Maintaining Aspect Ratio:

- Proportional Resizing: Hold the "Shift" key while resizing a logo to keep its aspect ratio intact, preventing distortion.

Precise Positioning:

- Using Alignment Tools: Utilize alignment tools to position logos accurately within frames. Snap to grid or use layout grids for consistent placement.

Styling Logos:

Applying Effects:

- Enhancing Appearance: Add effects like shadows, blurs, and overlays to logos for better integration or emphasis in your design.

Changing Colors:

- Editing SVG Logos: Adjust colors directly in Figma for SVG logos by selecting the logo and modifying the fill color in the properties panel.

Using Logos in Components:

Creating Components:

- Consistency Across Designs: Convert frequently used logos into components by selecting the logo and clicking "Create Component" in the toolbar.

Variants:

- Style Adaptations: Create different versions of logo components for various uses (e.g., light mode and dark mode). Variants allow easy switching between styles.

Exporting Logos:

Export Settings:

- Customizing Exports: Select the logo, adjust the export settings in the properties panel, and choose the format (PNG, JPG, SVG) and scale (e.g., 1x, 2x).

Batch Export:

- Multiple Assets: Use Figma's batch export feature to streamline exporting multiple logos or assets at once.

By mastering the use of frames and logos in Figma, you can create organized, professional designs that are easy to manage and maintain, ensuring consistency and high quality across all your projects.

Using Vector Tools and Design Elements

Figma offers a comprehensive set of vector tools and design elements essential for creating intricate and scalable designs. Here's a detailed guide on effectively utilizing these features:

Vector Tools in Figma:

Pen Tool:

- Creating and Editing Paths: Use the Pen tool (shortcut "P") to draw custom shapes and paths. Click to create points and segments, and click and drag to create curves. Modify points and curves using the Direct Selection tool (shortcut "A").

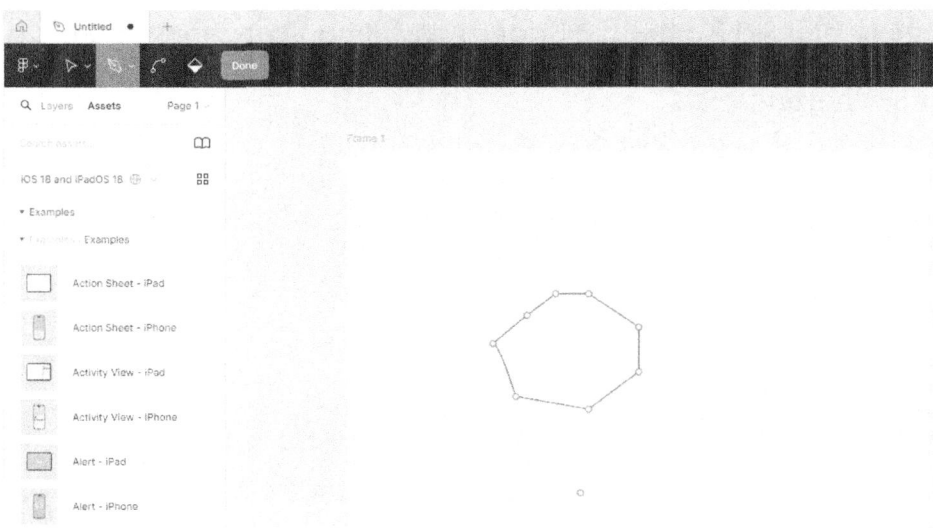

Shape Tools:

- Drawing and Adjusting Shapes: Utilize the Rectangle (R), Ellipse (O), Line (L), and Polygon tools to draw basic shapes. Drag on the canvas to set their dimensions. Adjust shapes by dragging edges or corners, and apply corner radius handles for rounded corners.

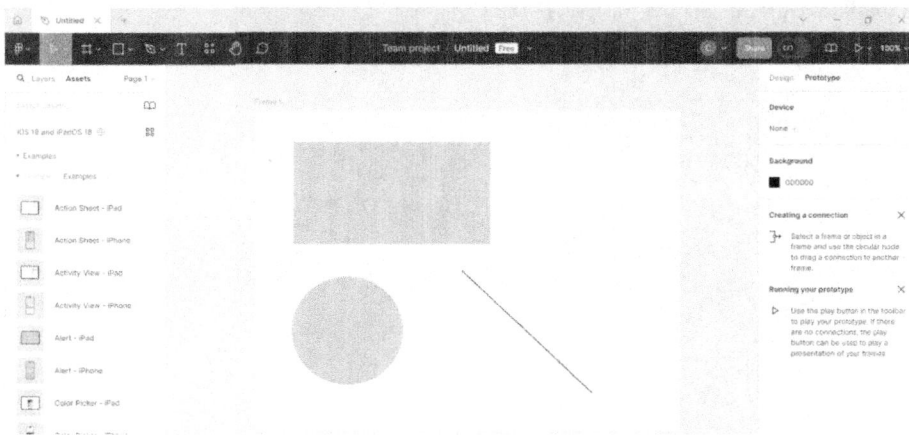

Boolean Operations:

- Combining Shapes: Merge basic shapes using Union, Subtract, Intersect, and Exclude operations. Select shapes, right-click, and choose the desired boolean operation to create complex shapes.

Vector Networks:

- Creating Non-linear Paths: Vector networks enable the creation of intricate, non-linear paths. Use the Pen tool to craft and refine these paths dynamically.

Vector Editing Shortcuts:

- Efficient Editing: Enhance workflow with shortcuts like holding "Shift" to maintain proportions or angles, and "Alt" to resize shapes from the center.

Design Elements in Figma:

Text Tool:

- Adding and Styling Text: Select the Text tool (shortcut "T") to insert text boxes on the canvas. Customize font, size, weight, color, alignment, and more in the properties panel for consistent styling.

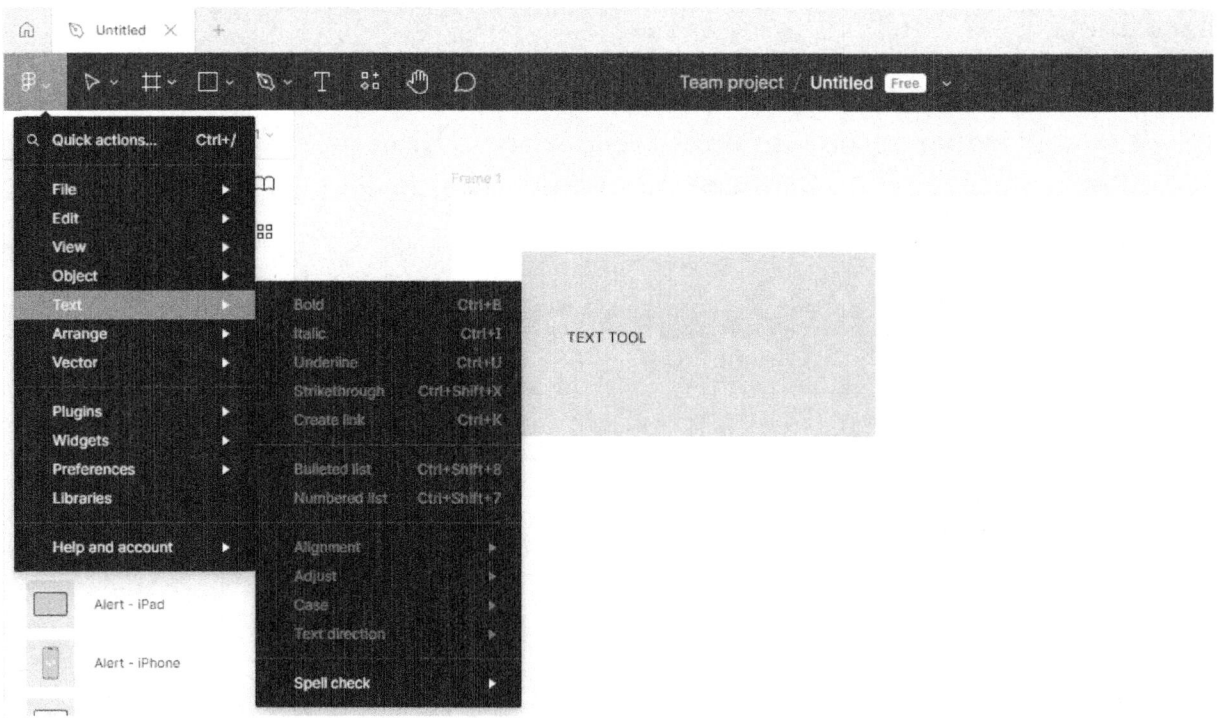

Images:
- Placing and Editing Images: Drag and drop image files (PNG, JPG, GIF) onto the canvas or use the "Place Image" tool. Adjust image properties such as opacity, fill, and effects. Use the crop tool to refine dimensions.

Components:
- Creating and Using Components: Convert frequently used design elements into reusable components with the "Create Component" option in the toolbar. Drag components from the Assets panel for easy integration across designs.

Component Variants:
- Designing with Variants: Create different versions or states of components using variants, ideal for interactive elements like buttons or forms.

Icons:
- Using and Customizing Icons: Import icon libraries or create custom icons using vector tools. Customize icon size, color, and stroke to align with design specifications.

Auto Layout:
- Building Responsive Layouts: Employ Auto Layout to design adaptive elements. Add Auto Layout to frames, adjusting padding, spacing, and alignment to ensure responsiveness across different content sizes.

Grids and Layouts:
- Applying Grids and Guides: Establish layout grids for consistent spacing and alignment within frames. Utilize guides from the rulers for precise element positioning on the canvas.

Mastering Figma's vector tools and design elements empowers you to create polished, scalable designs that excel in both visual appeal and functionality across various applications.

Text Styles, Topography and Text Editing

Figma's text tools offer extensive options for creating and editing text styles, ensuring your designs look great and are typographically consistent. Here's a comprehensive guide on effectively using Figma's text features:

Text Styles:

Creating Text Styles:

- Defining Styles: To create a text style, select a text layer with your chosen font, size, weight, color, and other properties. In the properties panel, click the four-dot icon next to the font section and select "Create Style." Name your style for easy reference.

- Applying Styles: Apply a text style by selecting a text layer and choosing from your predefined styles in the properties panel. This maintains design consistency.

Editing Text Styles:

- Updating Styles: To update a text style, select a text layer with the applied style, make your adjustments, and click the "Update" button in the styles panel. This will reflect changes in all instances of that text style across your project.

Typography:

Choosing Fonts:

- Font Selection: Figma supports a broad range of fonts. Use the Text tool (press "T") and select your desired font from the dropdown in the properties panel. You can use system fonts or upload custom fonts.

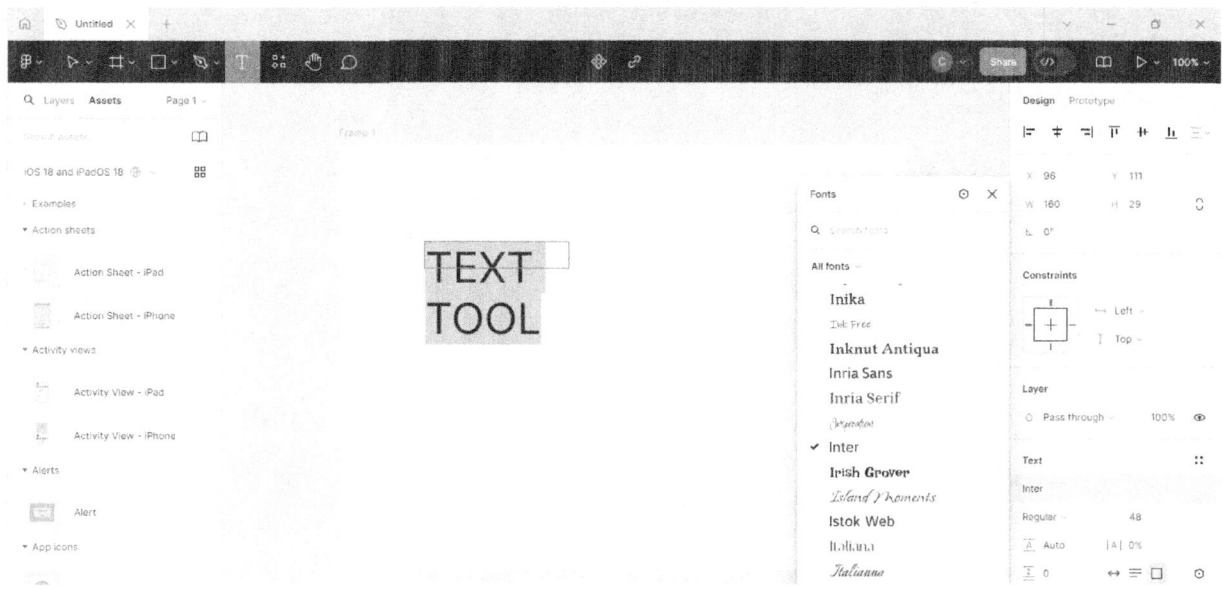

Font Properties:

- Adjusting Properties: Customize your text by adjusting font size, weight, line height, letter spacing, and paragraph spacing in the properties panel.

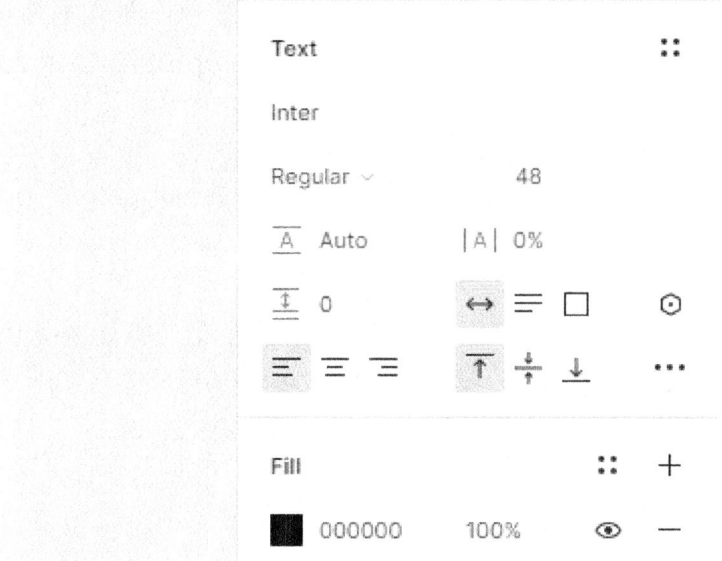

Advanced Typography:

- OpenType Features: Utilize OpenType features for advanced typographic control, such as ligatures, small caps, and alternate characters, accessible in the advanced typography settings.

Text Editing:

Basic Text Editing:

- Adding and Editing Text: Use the Text tool (press "T") to create a text box. Click on the canvas to type, or double-click an existing text box to edit it.

Formatting Text:

- In-line Formatting: Apply in-line formatting (bold, italic, underline) to specific parts of your text by selecting the text and using the formatting options in the properties panel or the right-click context menu.

Aligning Text:

- Text Alignment: Align text within a text box using the alignment options in the properties panel. Align text to the left, center, right, or justify it. Adjust vertical alignment to position text at the top, middle, or bottom of the text box.

Text Boxes:

- Resizing and Wrapping: Resize text boxes by clicking and dragging the edges or corners. Enable or disable text wrapping to control text flow within the box.

Utilizing Text Styles and Typography in Design:

Consistency Across Projects:

- Maintaining Consistency: Use text styles to maintain typographic consistency across different screens and components. This is especially important in UI/UX design to enhance the user experience.

Global Styles:
- Applying Global Changes: Implement global text styles to quickly update typography across your entire project. This is useful for making broad changes, such as updating the primary font or adjusting overall text size.

Collaboration:
- Sharing Styles: Share text styles with your team to ensure everyone uses the same typographic settings. This can be done by creating a shared library or using team projects in Figma.

Mastering text styles, typography, and text editing in Figma allows you to create professional and cohesive designs. These tools enable precise control over your text elements, ensuring your design projects are both visually appealing and typographically sound.

Creating and Applying Colors, Fills and Effects

Figma offers robust tools for creating and applying colors, fills, and effects, which can significantly enhance your designs. Here's a comprehensive guide on how to use these features effectively:

Colors and Fills:

Creating Colors:
- Color Picker: Click on the color swatch in the properties panel after selecting any shape or text layer. Use the hue slider, color field, or input a hex code to choose your desired color.

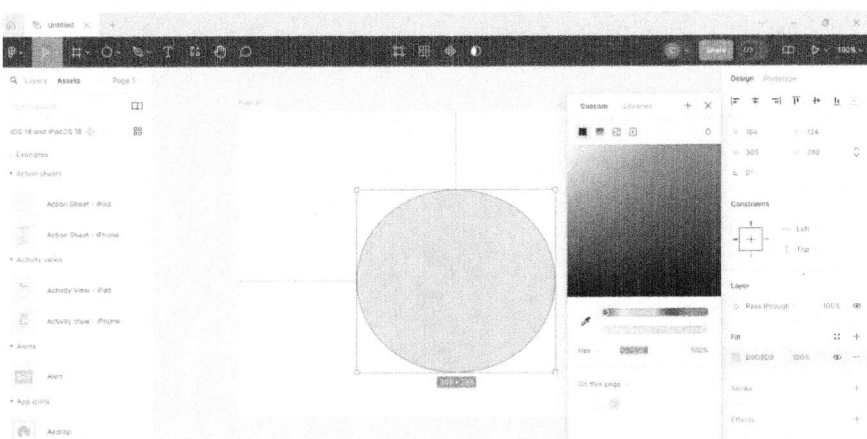

- Opacity and Blending: Adjust opacity to create transparency effects. Utilize blending modes like multiply, screen, or overlay for different visual effects.

Applying Fills:

- Solid Color Fills: Select the layer, click the fill swatch in the properties panel, and pick a color. This can be applied to shapes, text, and frames.
- Gradient Fills: Choose linear or radial gradients in the fill type from the color picker. Adjust the gradient stops and direction to achieve the desired look.
- Image Fills: Select the "Image" fill option to fill shapes with images. Upload an image and adjust its fit, crop, and position.

Effects:

Adding Effects:

- Shadows: Apply drop shadows or inner shadows to add depth. Customize the shadow's color, opacity, blur, spread, and offset in the effects panel.
- Blurs: Use layer blur or background blur for a soft, blurred effect. Adjust the blur radius to control the effect's intensity.
- Other Effects: Explore glows and overlays to enhance your design elements. Adjust settings like color, opacity, and spread to refine the effect.

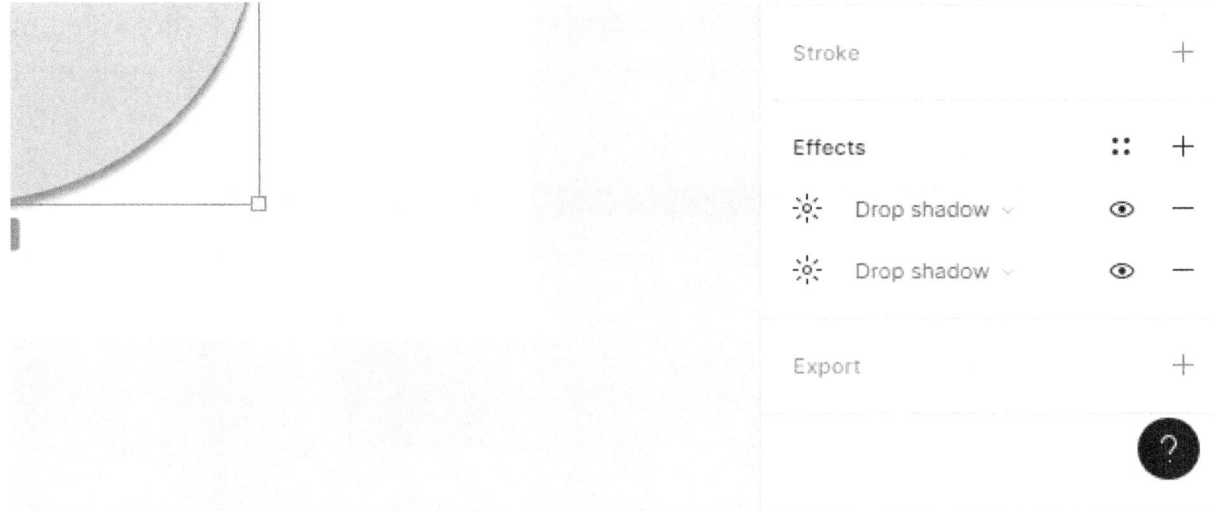

Color Styles:

Creating Color Styles:

- Define a Color Style: Select a layer with the desired color, click the four-dot icon next to the fill color in the properties panel, and choose "Create Style." Name the style for easy reference.

Applying Color Styles:

- Use Consistent Colors: Apply color styles by selecting a layer and choosing from your predefined styles in the properties panel, ensuring color consistency across your design.

Editing Color Styles:

- Update Styles: Modify a color style by selecting a layer with the applied style, changing the color, and clicking the "Update" button in the styles panel. This updates all instances of that color style in your project.

Advanced Techniques:

Using Color Palettes:

- Create Palettes: Develop color palettes by creating and saving multiple color styles to maintain a cohesive color scheme across your project.
- Share Palettes: Share your color palettes with team members by creating a shared library or using team projects, ensuring everyone uses the same colors.

Effects on Components:

- Consistent Effects: Apply effects to components to ensure uniformity. Effects applied to components will be consistent across different parts of your design.

Nested Effects:

- Complex Visuals: Combine multiple effects on a single layer to create intricate visuals. For example, use a mix of shadows, blurs, and overlays for a sophisticated look.

Best Practices:

Maintain Consistency:

- Global Styles: Use global color styles and effects to maintain consistency, simplifying updates across your entire project.

Optimize Performance:

- Minimize Effects: Use effects sparingly to avoid performance issues, as too many effects can slow down rendering and complicate file management.

Collaborate Efficiently:

- Shared Libraries: Use Figma's shared libraries to distribute color styles, gradients, and effects among your team, promoting a unified design approach.

By mastering Figma's tools for colors, fills, and effects, you can create visually appealing and cohesive designs. These features offer the flexibility to experiment with different styles and ensure your design elements are both aesthetically pleasing and functional.

CHAPTER FOUR
DESIGN SYSTEMS AND STYLE GUIDES

Establishing a Design System for Consistency

Figma lets you create a design system, a collection of reusable parts and rules that ensure your projects all look and work similarly. This guide will show you how to set up a powerful one:

What Exactly is a Design System?

Think of it as a toolbox for consistent UI building. It includes reusable components (buttons, forms, etc.), typography styles (fonts, sizes), colors, and spacing rules.

Why Bother with a Design System?

- Consistency: Everything looks and feels the same across your projects.
- Efficiency: No need to redesign the wheel – reuse existing components.
- Scalability: As your projects grow, so can your design system.
- Collaboration: Everyone on the team is on the same design page.

Building Your Design System Step-by-Step:

- Define Your Design Principles: What are the core ideas that will guide your design choices? (e.g., simplicity, accessibility)
- Craft a Style Guide: This is your design system's instruction manual. It should cover things like typography, colors, spacing, and icons.
- Develop Reusable Components: Design basic building blocks (buttons, inputs) and more complex ones (navigation bars, forms) using the basic ones.

Leverage Figma's Features:

- Component Libraries: Store reusable parts for easy access across projects.

- Shared Styles: Apply consistent colors, text styles, and effects throughout your designs.
- Auto Layout: Make components resize automatically for different screen sizes.
- Prototyping: Create interactive mockups to test how components work together.

Document Your Design System:

- Create a Guide: Explain how to use each component, style, and element.
- Include Examples: Show how to use the system in different situations.
- Version Control: Track changes to the system so everyone uses the latest version.

Collaboration is Important:

- Teamwork Makes the Dream Work: Involve designers, developers, and others in creating and maintaining the system.
- Regular Reviews: Get feedback and update the system as needed to keep it relevant.

By following these steps, you can establish a design system in Figma that keeps your projects consistent, efficient, and collaborative.

Creating and Managing Styles

Figma's powerful Styles feature allows you to streamline your design workflow and maintain a cohesive look across your projects. Here's how to create, manage, and apply styles effectively:

What are Styles?

Styles in Figma are like reusable paintbrushes for your design elements. They include sets of formatting options such as color, font, effects, and layout properties.

Applying a style instantly sets these properties for an element, ensuring consistency across your project.

Creating Styles:

Select an Element:

- Choose the element you want to define as a style (text, shape, frame, etc.).

Adjust Properties:

- Modify the desired properties (font, color, effects, etc.) in the properties panel on the right.

Create the Style:

- Click the "+" icon next to the "Style" section and name your style clearly and descriptively.

Benefits of Styles:

- Consistency: Ensures a uniform look and feel across your designs.
- Efficiency: Saves time by eliminating repetitive formatting tasks.
- Scalability: Easily update your design by changing a single style definition.
- Collaboration: Ensures all team members use the same styles.

Managing Styles:

Local vs. Library Styles:

- Figma offers local styles (specific to a project) and library styles (shared across projects). Organize them to maintain a clean workspace.

Editing Styles:

- Double-click on a style in the "Styles" panel to modify its properties. Changes will reflect in all elements using that style.

Reordering Styles:

- Drag and drop styles within the "Styles" panel to customize their order for easier access.

Applying Styles:

Style Picker:

- Select the element you want to style. Click the style dropdown menu in the properties panel and choose the desired style.

Overriding Styles:

- Customize individual properties of an element after applying a style. These changes won't affect the original style definition.

Tips:

- Descriptive Naming: Use clear and descriptive names for your styles to easily identify them later.
- Global Colors: Define core brand colors as global styles for consistent application throughout your designs.
- Component Styles: Create styles specifically for reusable components to maintain a unified look and feel.

Mastering Styles in Figma will help you enhance your design efficiency, ensure consistency, and establish a solid foundation for collaborative design projects.

Using Libraries and Components for Reusability

Figma's Libraries and Components are crucial for developing reusable design elements and maintaining uniformity across projects. Here's a detailed guide on how to effectively use these features:

Libraries in Figma:

Understanding Libraries:

- Libraries are collections of reusable assets like components, styles, and icons that can be shared across multiple files and projects. This promotes consistency and expedites the design process.

Creating a Library:

- Set Up a File: Start by creating a new Figma file to serve as your library.
- Add Assets: Design and add components, text styles, color styles, and other assets you plan to reuse.
- Publish the Library: In the file, go to the "Assets" panel, click on the library icon, and select "Publish." Name your library and choose which assets to include.

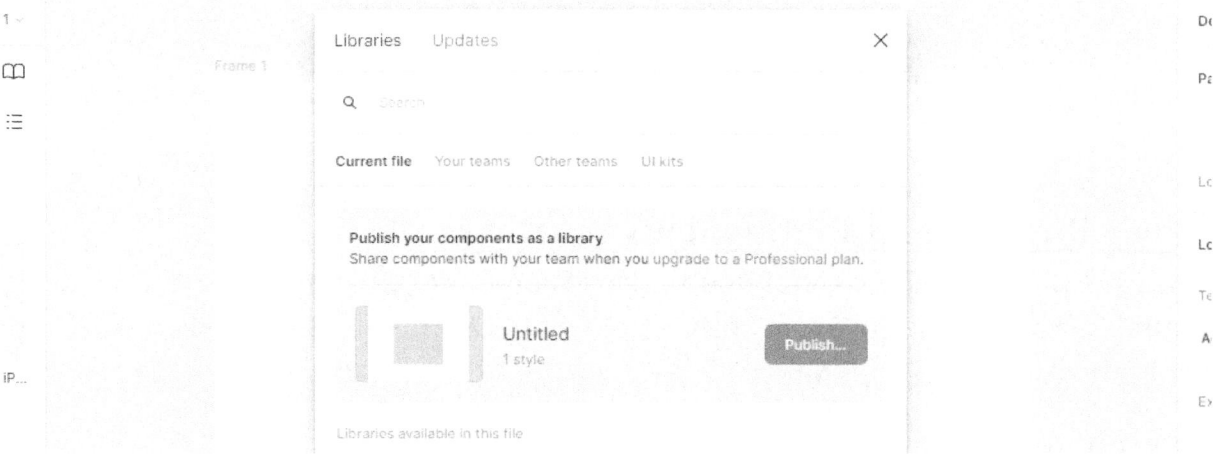

Using a Library:

- Enable the Library: In any Figma file, go to the "Assets" panel, click on the library icon, and toggle on the desired library.
- Insert Assets: Drag and drop components and styles from the library into your design file.

Components in Figma:

Understanding Components:

- Components are reusable design elements that help maintain consistency and save time. Any changes made to the master component automatically update all instances of that component.

Creating Components:

- Design the Element: Create the design element you want to reuse.
- Convert to Component: Select the element and click "Create Component" in the toolbar or right-click and select "Create Component."

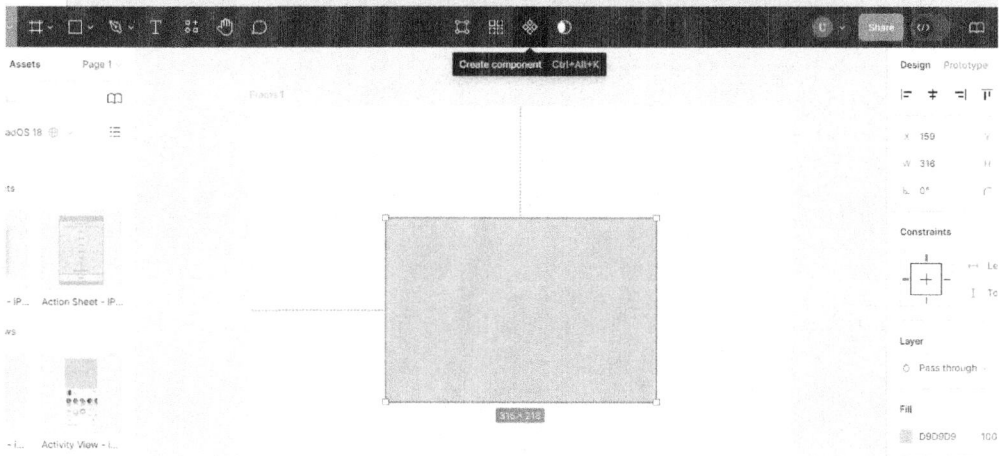

Using Components:

- Drag and Drop: Drag components from the "Assets" panel into your design.

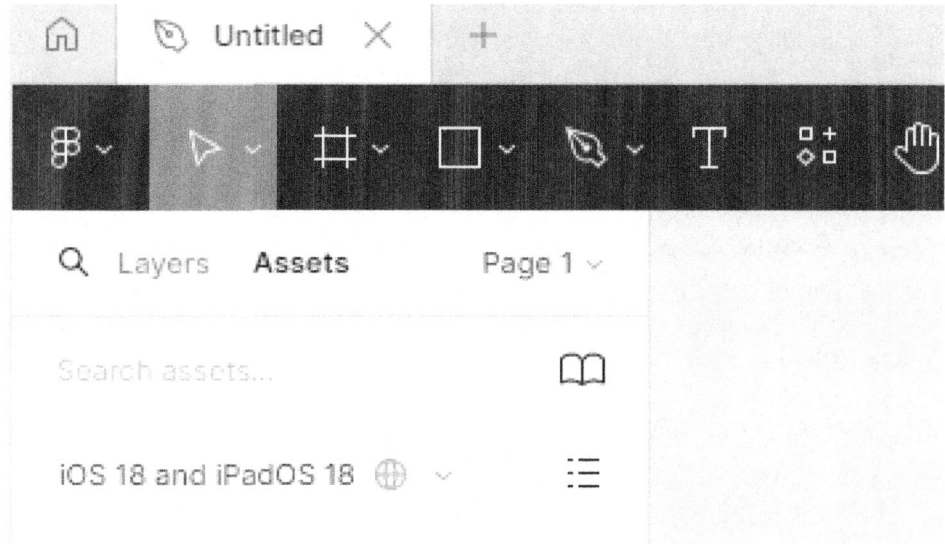

- Override Properties: Customize individual instances of a component by overriding properties like text or color without affecting the master component.

Component Variants:

- Create Variants: Design multiple versions of a component (e.g., buttons in different states). Select the component, click "Add Variant," and adjust the properties.

- Switch Between Variants: Use the properties panel to switch between different variants of a component in your design.

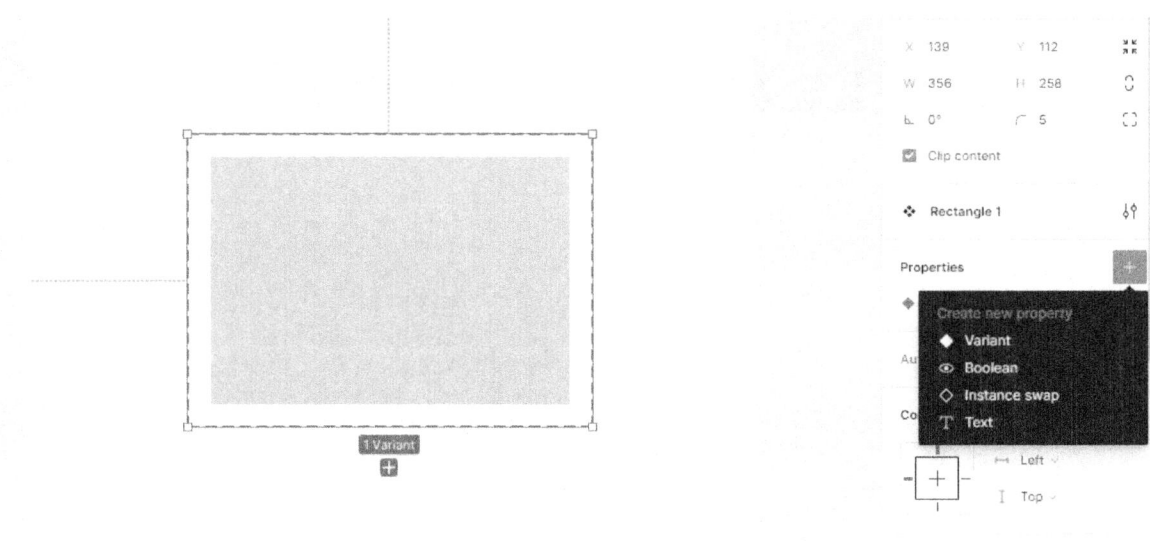

Best Practices for Reusability:

Organize Assets:

- Clear Naming Conventions: Use descriptive names for components and styles to easily identify and search for them.

- Categorize Assets: Group related components and styles into folders within the library for better organization.

Maintain Consistency:

- Global Styles: Use global styles for colors, text, and effects to ensure consistency across all components and projects.

- Update Regularly: Keep your libraries and components up-to-date to reflect the latest design standards and changes.

Collaborate Efficiently:

- Shared Libraries: Share libraries with team members to ensure everyone is using the same assets and styles.
- Feedback and Iteration: Collect feedback from your team and iterate on components and libraries to improve their usability and effectiveness.

By mastering Libraries and Components in Figma, you can build a scalable and efficient design system that ensures consistency and fosters collaboration. This enhances the quality of your designs and streamlines the design process, saving time and effort.

CHAPTER FIVE
BUILDING USER INTERFACE ELEMENTS

Designing Buttons, Icons and Input Fields

Figma offers a robust platform for creating and perfecting UI elements such as buttons, icons, and input fields. Here's a detailed approach to designing these essential components:

Designing Buttons:

Basic Button Design:

- Create the Shape: Use the Rectangle tool ("R") to draw the foundation of the button. Resize it according to your needs.

- Add Text: Utilize the Text tool ("T") to add the button label. Center the text within the button shape.

- Style the Button: Adjust the button's fill color, border radius, and text style in the properties panel. Ensure readability and visual appeal.

Advanced Button States:

- Hover and Active States: Duplicate the base button and alter its fill color, border, or shadow to create distinct hover and active states.

- Disabled State: Create a disabled version by reducing opacity or choosing a muted color palette to indicate inactivity.

Creating Button Components:

- Make a Component: Select the button and its label, then click "Create Component" in the toolbar or right-click and choose "Create Component."

- Add Variants: Use the Variants feature to incorporate different button states (default, hover, active, disabled) within the same component.

Designing Icons:

Basic Icon Design:

- Utilize Vector Tools: Use Figma's vector tools like the Pen tool ("P"), Shape tools, and Boolean operations to create custom icons.
- Ensure Consistency: Maintain a consistent style across your icons, including stroke width, corner radius, and overall size.

Managing Icon Libraries:

- Import Icons: Drag and drop icon files (SVG, PNG) into your Figma project. Arrange them in the "Assets" panel.
- Create Icon Components: Convert icons into components for easy reuse. Group similar icons together for better organization.

Customizing Icons:

- Adjust Size and Color: Scale icons proportionally and modify their color to align with your design scheme.
- Apply Effects: Add shadows or blurs to icons to enhance depth and emphasis.

Designing Input Fields:

Basic Input Field Design:

- Create the Shape: Use the Rectangle tool ("R") to draw the input field's base shape. Adjust its dimensions to fit the form.
- Add Placeholder Text: Use the Text tool ("T") to add placeholder text. Center it within the input field.
- Style the Input Field: Customize the border, fill color, and text style in the properties panel. Make sure the placeholder text is distinguishable from the actual input text.

Advanced Input States:

- Focus and Error States: Duplicate the base input field and change the border color or shadow to create focus and error states.

- Disabled State:
- Create a disabled version by lowering opacity or selecting a muted color scheme.

Creating Input Field Components:

- Make a Component: Select the input field and placeholder text, then click "Create Component" in the toolbar or right-click and select "Create Component."
- Add Variants: Use the Variants feature to incorporate different input states (default, focus, error, disabled) within the same component.

Best Practices for UI Elements:

Consistency:

- Maintain Uniformity: Ensure that buttons, icons, and input fields follow a consistent style guide to enhance the user experience.
- Apply Styles: Use global styles for colors, text, and effects to maintain consistency across all UI elements.

Accessibility:

- Ensure Legibility: Make sure button labels and input field text are easily readable.
- Design Clear Icons: Create icons that are easily recognizable and intuitive.

Usability:

- Provide Interactive Feedback: Offer visual feedback for button and input field interactions to enhance user engagement.
- Handle Errors Clearly: Indicate input field errors clearly to guide users in correcting their entries.

Mastering the design of buttons, icons, and input fields in Figma allows you to create intuitive and visually appealing interfaces that improve user experience and maintain consistency across your projects.

Creating Navigating Bars, Menus and Dropdowns

Here's a detailed guide on creating navigation bars, menus, and dropdowns in Figma:

Navigation Bars:

Create a Frame:

- Begin by creating a new frame where you intend to place your navigation bar. Use the frame tool (F) to draw a rectangle at the top or bottom of your design canvas.

Design the Layout:

- Determine the structure and layout of your navigation bar, including the placement and number of navigation items (links or buttons).

Add Navigation Items:

- Utilize text layers (T key) or shape layers to create buttons or links for each navigation item. Ensure they are evenly spaced and aligned within the navigation bar.

Style Navigation Items:

- Customize the appearance of each navigation item, adjusting font style, size, color, and incorporating hover effects to signify interactivity.

Group and Componentize:

- Select all navigation items and group them (Cmd/Ctrl + G). Convert the grouped items into a component (Cmd/Ctrl + Alt + K) to facilitate reuse and management across your design.

Menus:

Design the Menu Container:

- Create a new frame or use an existing one to house the menu. Decide on the menu's orientation—vertical or horizontal—based on your design needs.

Add Menu Items:

- Design individual menu items as buttons or text links within the menu frame. Consider including icons alongside text for clarity and visual appeal.

Implement Dropdown Functionality:

- Introduce dropdown functionality by either designing nested frames for sub-menus or utilizing Figma's interactive components to create hover or click interactions that reveal additional content.

Style and Customize:

- Customize the appearance of menu items and dropdowns with appropriate spacing, borders, shadows, and animations to enhance user interaction and visual appeal.

Dropdowns:

Design the Dropdown Component:

- Create a clickable area for the dropdown by drawing a rectangle or shape. Ensure it is sufficiently sized to accommodate the dropdown content.

Add Dropdown Content:

- Design the content that appears when the dropdown is activated, such as text, icons, or interactive elements.

Interactive States:

- Design interactive states like hover effects or animations to provide visual feedback when users interact with the dropdown.

Group and Componentize:

- Group all dropdown elements (clickable area and content) and convert them into a component for easy reuse and management across different sections of your design.

Best Practices:

- Consistency: Maintain consistent design patterns, spacing, and typography across navigation bars, menus, and dropdowns.

- Accessibility: Ensure components are accessible via keyboard navigation and provide clear visual cues for interactive elements.

- User Testing: Conduct usability tests with real users to ensure navigation components are intuitive and functional.

- Responsive Design: Design components to be responsive, adapting seamlessly to various screen sizes and orientations.

By following these steps and best practices, you can effectively create intuitive and functional navigation bars, menus, and dropdowns in Figma, enhancing user navigation and interaction within your designs.

Creating Variants for Different Design States

Figma equips you with the tools to design user-friendly forms, dialogs, and modals, fostering effective user interaction and data collection within your interfaces. Here's an extensive guide on working with forms, dialogs, and modals in Figma:

Forms:

Creating a Frame:

- Start by creating a new frame where your form will reside. Use the frame tool (shortcut: F) to draw a rectangle or any desired shape on your canvas.

Designing Form Elements:

- Utilize text layers (shortcut: T) for labels, input fields (like rectangles for text input areas), checkboxes, radio buttons, and any other necessary form components. Ensure precise alignment and spacing for clarity and usability.

Styling Form Elements:

- Customize the appearance of form elements such as input fields (including placeholders and borders), buttons, checkboxes, and dropdowns. Maintain consistency in typography, colors, and spacing to achieve a cohesive design.

Grouping and Componentizing:

- Group related form elements together (Cmd/Ctrl + G) and convert them into components (Cmd/Ctrl + Alt + K) for streamlined reuse across different parts of your design. This approach enhances consistency and optimizes workflow efficiency.

Dialogs:

Designing the Dialog Container:

- Create a new frame or utilize an existing one for the dialog box. Determine its size and position relative to your primary content or interface.

Adding Dialog Elements:

- Design elements within the dialog, including titles, text content, buttons (e.g., "OK", "Cancel"), icons for clarity, and any interactive components essential for user actions.

Styling and Customization:

- Customize the appearance of the dialog box by adjusting properties like borders, shadows, background colors, and opacity. These adjustments help differentiate the dialog from the main interface, guiding users' focus to the dialog's content.

Interactive States:

- Define interactive states for buttons and links within the dialog to provide visual feedback when users interact with them. Employ subtle animations or color changes to signify interactivity effectively.

Modals:

Creating the Modal Container:

- Draw a rectangle or shape to serve as the background container for your modal. Ensure it covers the main interface to emphasize the modal's transient nature and significance.

Designing Modal Content:

- Create the modal content, including titles, messages, input fields, buttons, or any other interactive elements needed for user interaction or input.

Styling and Animation:

- Apply styles such as gradients, shadows, or opacity adjustments to distinguish the modal from the background interface. Consider incorporating animations or transitions to enhance the modal's visual appeal and user experience.

Best Practices:

- Consistency: Maintain uniform design patterns, spacing, alignment, and typography across all forms, dialogs, and modals. Consistency enhances visual coherence and usability.

- Accessibility: Ensure all interactive elements are accessible via keyboard navigation (tab order) and provide clear visual cues (focus states, contrast) for users with disabilities.

- User Feedback: Implement feedback mechanisms within forms, dialogs, and modals to guide users in their interactions. Utilize error messages, tooltips, or success indicators to enhance user experience.

- Responsive Design: Design components to be responsive, adjusting seamlessly to various screen sizes and orientations. Test designs across different devices to ensure elements adapt appropriately.

Designing Interactive Elements and Microinteractions

Creating interactive elements and microinteractions in Figma involves crafting compelling user experiences through subtle animations and responsive feedback. Here's a comprehensive approach to designing these components effectively:

Interactive Elements:

Choosing Elements:

- Select the elements you wish to make interactive, such as buttons, links, sliders, or cards, ensuring clarity in their design.

Defining Interactions:

- Determine the various interactive states for each element (e.g., default, hover, active) and plan visual changes to provide user feedback.

Implementing Interactivity:

- Utilize Figma's prototyping tools to define interactions, including hover effects, click animations, or state transitions.

Animation and Timing:

- Integrate animations to enhance interaction clarity and visual appeal, adjusting timing and easing for smooth transitions.

Feedback Mechanisms:

- Provide clear visual cues and feedback through animations, color adjustments, or microinteractions to signify user interaction.

Microinteractions:

Identifying Opportunities:

- Identify key moments where microinteractions can improve usability or delight users, such as button presses or form validations.

Designing Microinteractions:

- Craft subtle yet meaningful microinteractions, like loading spinners, success animations, or error indicators within forms or buttons.

Prototyping Microinteractions:

- Use Figma's prototyping capabilities to simulate microinteractions, defining triggers (e.g., hover, click) and specifying responses (animations, state changes).

Testing and Refinement:

- Conduct usability tests with real users to ensure intuitive interactions and gather feedback to refine animations and timing.

Best Practices:

- Usability: Ensure interactive elements and microinteractions enhance rather than detract from the user experience, keeping animations functional and subtle.

- Consistency: Maintain consistent design patterns and interaction behaviors across your project to foster a cohesive user interface.

- Performance: Optimize animations and interactions for smooth responsiveness, especially for web and mobile applications.

- Feedback Loop: Incorporate user feedback to iterate on interactive elements and microinteractions, continuously improving usability and engagement.

By following these detailed guidelines and best practices in Figma, you can effectively design interactive elements and microinteractions that not only enhance usability but also create engaging user experiences within your designs.

CHAPTER SIX
ADVANCED DESIGN TECHNIQUES IN FIGMA

Grids, Layouts and Auto Layout for Responsive Design

Utilizing grids, layouts, and auto layout in Figma is essential for crafting responsive designs that seamlessly adjust to diverse screen sizes and orientations. Here's a detailed guide on harnessing these features effectively:

Grids in Figma:

Understanding Grids:

- Grids establish a structured framework to organize content, ensuring alignment and consistency across design elements. They involve columns and rows that dictate spacing and proportions within a layout.

Setting Up Grids:

- Define Grid Settings: Specify parameters like column width, gutter width, and alignment.

- Applying Grids: Utilize grids to consistently align and position elements throughout your design.

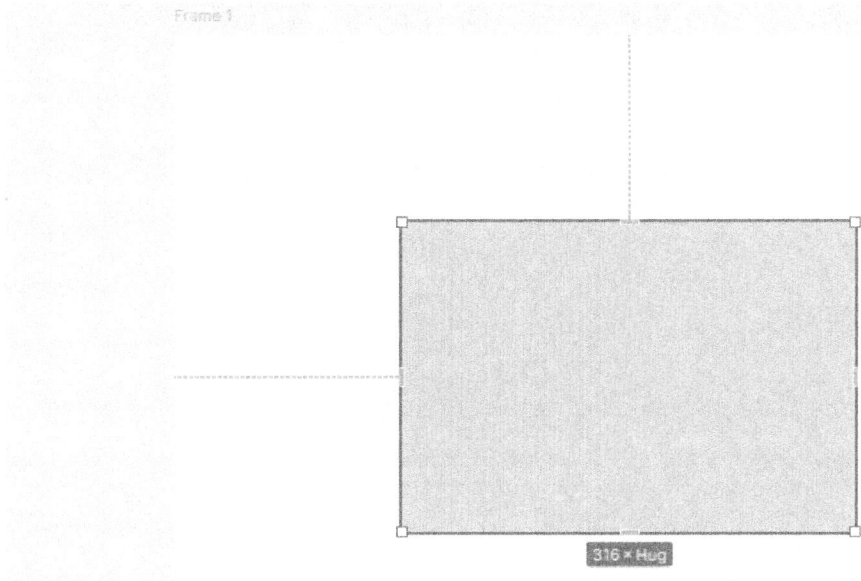

Responsive Grids:

- Adjust grid configurations to suit different screen sizes and orientations, maintaining visual harmony.

Layouts in Figma:

Flexible Layout Options:

- Figma offers diverse methods to arrange and manage elements within frames and components.

Manual Layout:

- Positioning Elements: Arrange elements manually by dragging them within a frame.
- Fine-tuning Spacing: Use alignment guides and spacing tools to refine the placement of elements.

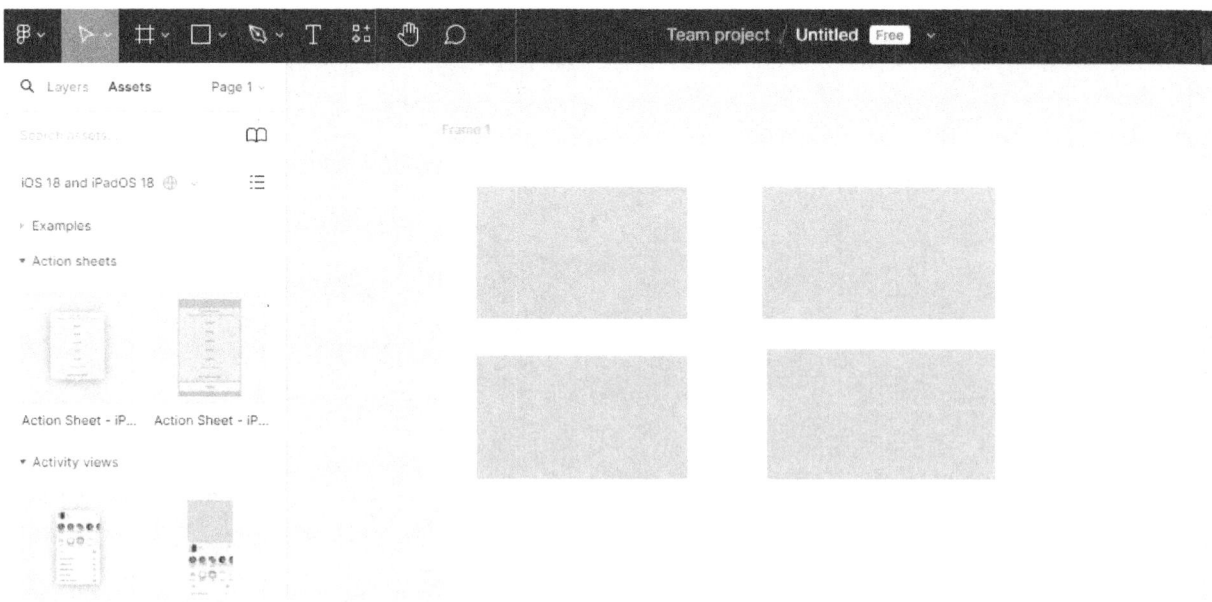

Auto Layout in Figma:

Automated Flexibility:

- Auto layout simplifies responsive design by automatically resizing and repositioning elements based on content adjustments.

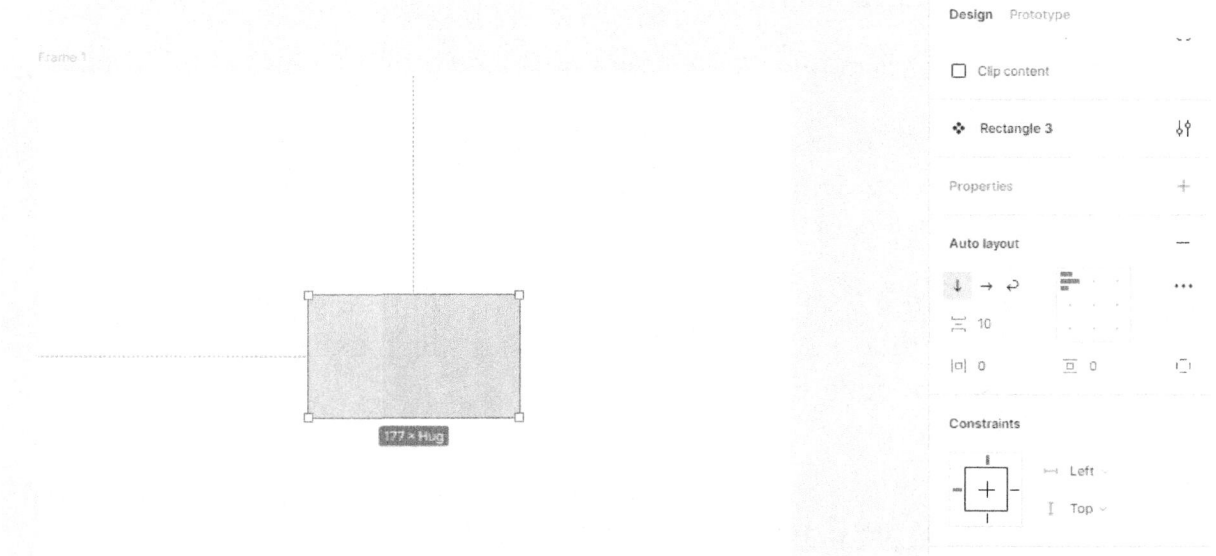

Key Features:

- Enabling Auto Layout: Activate auto layout within frames to dynamically adjust elements as content changes.
- Padding and Spacing: Define internal padding and spacing within an auto layout frame to ensure consistent element spacing.

Benefits of Responsive Design:

- Efficiency: Save time by automating layout adjustments for different screen sizes.
- Consistency: Maintain alignment and spacing consistency across various devices.
- Scalability: Easily update and refine designs without manual adjustments for each element.

Best Practices for Responsive Design:

- Planning for Variability: Consider how designs will adapt across different screen sizes and orientations.

- Consistent Spacing: Maintain uniform spacing and alignment guidelines across all layouts and grids.

- Device Testing: Preview designs on multiple devices to ensure responsiveness and usability.

- Documenting Guidelines: Create documentation outlining grid systems, layout principles, and auto layout usage for team reference.

Mastering grids, layouts, and auto layout in Figma empowers you to create responsive designs that scale effectively across devices, enhancing both user experience and design coherence.

Using Constraints and Resizing for Design Flexibility

Using Constraints and Resizing in Figma offers crucial design flexibility to ensure your designs adjust effectively to various screen sizes and layout changes. Here's a detailed guide on utilizing these features in Figma:

Constraints in Figma:

Understanding Constraints:

- Constraints in Figma dictate how objects behave when their parent frames are resized, controlling their position and size relative to their containers.

Applying Constraints:

- Select an Object: Choose the object you wish to apply constraints to, such as a button or an icon.

- Access the Constraints Panel: Locate and open the Constraints panel from the properties panel or the right-click menu.

- Setting Constraints: Horizontal Constraints: Define how the object behaves along the X-axis (left, center, right).

- Vertical Constraints: Specify how the object behaves along the Y-axis (top, center, bottom).

- Aspect Ratio Constraints: Maintain the object's aspect ratio to prevent distortion when resized.

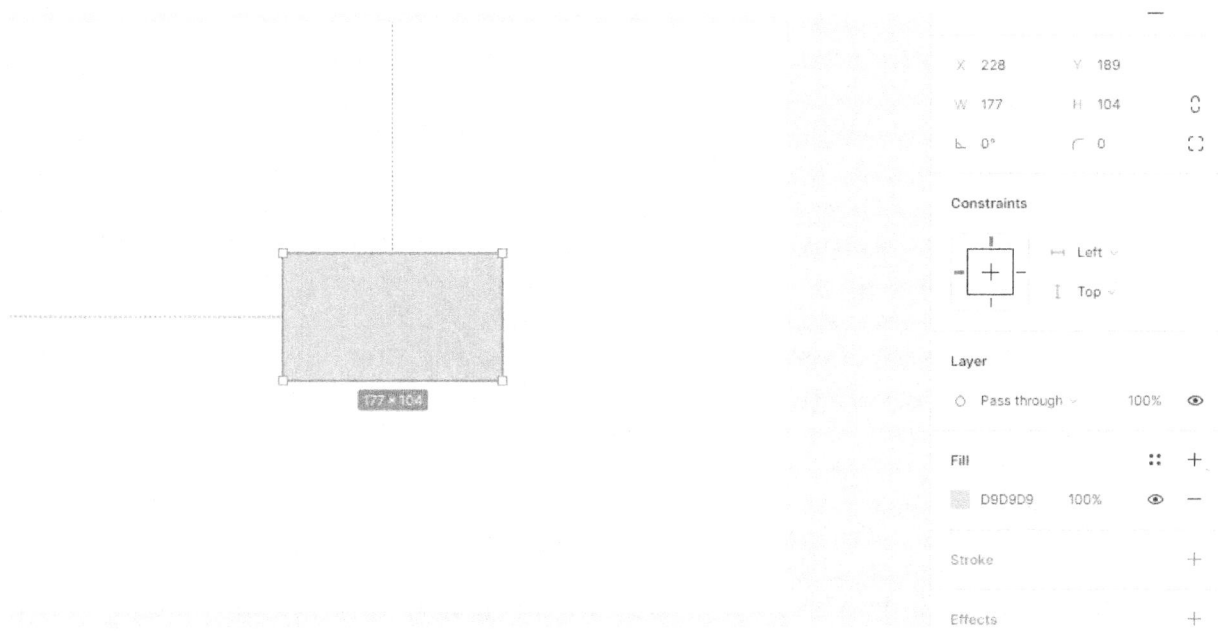

Adjust Resizing Behavior:

- Fill: Stretches the object to fill its container while maintaining its aspect ratio if specified.

- Fit: Resizes the object to fit within its container without stretching.

- Horizontal and Vertical Scaling: Control whether the object scales horizontally, vertically, or both.

Preview and Adjustment:

- Use the resizing handles on the parent frame to preview how the object responds to resizing scenarios.

- Fine-tune constraints and resizing settings until achieving the desired behavior.

Resizing Techniques in Figma:

Manual Resizing:

- Select the Object: Choose the object you want to resize, such as a text box, shape, or component.
- Adjust Size: Use corner handles for proportional resizing.
  - Use side handles for resizing along a single axis (horizontal or vertical).
- Maintain Aspect Ratio: Hold the Shift key while resizing to maintain the object's aspect ratio.
  - Adjust size constraints and aspect ratio settings in the properties panel for precise control.

Best Practices for Constraints and Resizing:

- Plan Ahead: Consider various screen sizes and orientations during initial design phases.
- Use Constraints Strategically: Maintain relative positioning and scalability of design elements by applying constraints judiciously.
- Test Responsiveness: Preview designs across different devices and screen sizes to ensure optimal responsiveness.
- Document Guidelines: Create documentation or guidelines to facilitate effective use of constraints and resizing techniques among team members.
- Iterate Based on Feedback: Gather feedback from stakeholders and users to refine resizing behaviors for improved user experience.

Mastering constraints and resizing techniques in Figma empowers you to create adaptable and cohesive designs that enhance usability and visual consistency across diverse projects and devices.

Creating Variants for Different Design States

What are Variants?

Variants allow you to create a single UI component that can change its appearance based on user interaction or different properties like size and color. This feature simplifies managing multiple states within one component.

Creating Variants:

Designing the Base Component:

Create the Core Component: Develop the initial version of your component, such as a default button, which serves as the foundation for all variations.

Adding Variants:

- Select the Component: Click on the component to access its properties panel in Figma.

- Access Variants: Locate the "Variants" section in the properties panel, often marked by a diamond icon. Click the "+" icon to add a new variant.

- Define Variant Properties: Choose a property to vary (e.g., fill color, border radius) from the dropdown menu. Adjust the property value to create a new state for the component (e.g., hover state with a darker fill color).

Creating Additional States:

- Repeat the Process: Follow the steps to define more variants for other interaction states (like active, disabled) or different property variations (such as varying sizes).

Benefits of Using Variants:

- Efficiency: Saves time by eliminating the need to design multiple versions of the same component separately for different states.

- Consistency: Ensures all variants of a component maintain the same design standards, promoting a cohesive look and feel.

- Scalability: Easily expand or modify existing variants as your design requirements evolve.

- Organization: Keeps your design assets tidy by grouping all variations under a single component.

Advanced Use Cases:

- Complex Interactions: Design variants for interactive elements like hover effects, toggle states, or progress indicators.

- Responsive Design: Manage size variations within the same variant set to accommodate different screen sizes (e.g., mobile vs. desktop).

- Content Variations: Utilize variants for components that display different content based on context, such as cards with active and inactive states.

Bonus Tip:

Descriptive Naming: Assign clear and descriptive names to your variants to easily identify them within your design project.

Design for Accessibility in Figma

Creating accessible designs in Figma involves making interfaces usable for individuals with diverse abilities. Here's a guide on how to approach accessibility in your Figma designs:

Understanding Accessibility in Figma:

What is Accessibility?

- Accessibility ensures that your designs are functional for people with disabilities, encompassing visual, auditory, motor, and cognitive impairments. It aims to create inclusive user experiences.

Design Considerations for Accessibility:

Color Contrast:

- High Contrast: Ensure text and background colors have sufficient contrast for readability by users with low vision. Use tools like Figma's color picker to verify contrast ratios.

Text Legibility:
- Readable Fonts: Choose fonts that are clear and maintain proper spacing between characters. Avoid overly decorative or script fonts for body text.

Typography Settings:
- Font Size: Use a minimum font size of 12 points for body text to ensure readability. Allow users to resize text without affecting layout or functionality.

Focus States:
- Visible Focus: Design distinct focus states for interactive elements like buttons and links. Ensure they are noticeable for keyboard users navigating the interface.

Keyboard Accessibility:
- Navigable Interface: Ensure all interactive elements can be accessed and operated using a keyboard alone. Use Figma's prototyping tools to simulate keyboard navigation.

Alternative Text:
- Image Descriptions: Provide descriptive alt text for images and icons to assist users who rely on screen readers. Include pertinent details that convey the image's purpose.

Form Fields and Labels:
- Accessible Forms: Associate labels with form fields using Figma's auto layout and constraints to maintain alignment. Clearly mark required fields and provide helpful error messages.

Implementing Accessibility in Figma:

Design with Accessibility Guidelines:
- WCAG Compliance: Adhere to Web Content Accessibility Guidelines (WCAG) to ensure your designs meet international accessibility standards. Utilize color contrast checkers and accessibility plugins within Figma.

Collaboration and Feedback:

- User Testing: Conduct usability tests with people who have disabilities to gather feedback on accessibility. Utilize Figma's collaboration features to share prototypes and collect insights.

Documentation and Guidelines:

- Accessibility Guidelines: Create documentation outlining accessibility requirements and best practices for your design team. Use Figma's commenting and documentation features to communicate accessibility considerations.

Benefits of Designing for Accessibility:

- Inclusivity: Ensures your designs are usable by a wider audience, including individuals with disabilities.

- Legal Compliance: Helps meet legal requirements and standards for accessibility in different regions.

- Enhanced User Experience: Improves usability for all users, leading to increased engagement and satisfaction.

By integrating accessibility principles into your Figma design process, you can create interfaces that are inclusive and user-friendly for everyone. This approach not only enhances usability but also aligns with ethical and legal standards, fostering a positive user experience across your projects.

CHAPTER SEVEN
PROTOTYPING BASICS AND TECHNIQUES

Introduction to Prototyping in Figma

Figma's prototyping feature lets you create interactive mockups that simulate how users will experience your design. It's more than just static images - you can define how users navigate, interact with elements, and see animations.

Building Blocks of Figma Prototypes:

- Frames: These are like containers that hold your design elements, like buttons and text.

- Interactive Elements: Buttons, links, and input fields are what users can click or tap on in your prototype.

- States and Transitions: Imagine different appearances for an element (e.g., a button that looks normal, then pressed, then released). Transitions define how elements smoothly change between these states, sometimes with animations.

- Hotspots: These are invisible areas you place on your design that users can click or tap on. They trigger actions like moving to a different screen.

Steps to Prototype in Figma:

- Design Your Screens: Build your interface using frames or artboards in Figma.

- Define How Elements Behave: Decide how elements like buttons change when clicked or hovered over.

- Add Interactive Elements: Place buttons, links, and other interactive elements on your screens.

- Set Up Transitions: Tell Figma how elements should move between screens when users interact with them. You can even add animations for a polished look.

- Create User Journeys: Link your screens together using hotspots to show how users navigate through your design.

- Test and Refine: Use Figma's preview mode to interact with your prototype like a user would. Get feedback and make changes based on how well it works.

Why Prototype in Figma?

- Clearer Communication: Prototypes are more engaging than static images, making it easier to explain your design ideas to others.

- Early User Feedback: Test your design with real people early on to identify any usability issues before you invest too much time in development.

- Easy Iteration: Since prototypes are digital, it's simple to make changes based on feedback. No need to start from scratch.

Connecting Frames and Creating User Flows

Connecting frames and establishing user flows in Figma is crucial for crafting interactive prototypes that mimic user navigation within your interface. Here's an in-depth guide on how to connect frames and build user flows effectively in Figma:

Connecting Frames:

Prepare Your Frames:

- Ensure all necessary frames or artboards are set up in your Figma file, each representing different screens or states in your application or website.

Navigate to Prototype Mode:

- Switch to Prototype mode by clicking on the "Prototype" tab at the top right of the Figma interface or using the shortcut key (Shift + Command/Ctrl + P).

Select an Element:

- Click on the element within your frame that you intend to make interactive, such as a button, link, or any clickable area triggering user actions.

Create a Connection:

- Drag the blue connector arrow that appears from the selected element toward the destination frame. This action defines how users will interact and transition between screens.

Define Trigger and Action:

- Release the connector arrow over the destination frame to set up a modal. Here, specify the trigger (e.g., click, hover) and action (e.g., navigate to a new frame, open overlay) for the interaction.

Adjust Transition Options:

- Customize transition settings like animation type (e.g., slide, dissolve), easing (e.g., ease-in-out), and duration to refine how transitions behave. This enhances the prototype's realism and user experience.

Create Multiple Connections:

- Repeat the process to link other interactive elements to different frames. This method enables you to map out comprehensive user flows that simulate real-world navigation scenarios.

Creating User Flows:

Map Out User Paths:

- Before connecting frames, map user paths or flows within your application. Consider various scenarios to determine how users will navigate between screens based on their interactions.

Use Hotspots for Navigation:

- Utilize hotspots, invisible interactive areas placed on frames, to simulate navigation between frames not directly connected by interactive elements. This method enhances prototype functionality.

Organize and Label Connections:

- Maintain prototype organization by clearly labeling connections with descriptive names or actions. This practice facilitates easier understanding of interaction flows during testing and review.

Test User Flows:

- Preview your prototype in Figma's Preview mode to simulate user interaction and navigate through defined user flows. Identify potential usability issues, navigation errors, or areas requiring improvement.

Iterate Based on Feedback:

- Gather feedback from stakeholders, team members, or prototype users to refine user flows. Adjust connections, transitions, or screen layouts based on insights gathered during testing phases.

Benefits of Connecting Frames and Creating User Flows in Figma:

Visualize Navigation Paths:

- Clearly depict and communicate how users will navigate through your interface design.

Validate Design Decisions:

- Test and validate user flows early in the design process to enhance usability and overall user experience.

Iterative Improvement:

- Facilitate iterative design improvements based on user feedback and testing results, refining interactions and transitions effectively.

7.1 Prototyping Interactions and Animation

Prototypes in Figma are interactive designs.

Every prototype begins with a single interaction. Each interaction consists of a trigger, which initiates the interaction, and an action, which is the result of the trigger.

Certain interactions occur on a single object. For example:

- Clicking an object to open an external URL.
- Clicking a video to play or pause it.

Other interactions occur between two objects or frames and are considered connections. For instance:

- Clicking a button to navigate to another frame.
- Clicking an object to open an overlay.

A prototype connection is composed of three main components:

- Hotspot: This is where the interaction happens. A hotspot can be the frame itself or any object within it, such as a button, icon, or heading.

- Connection: The connector arrow that links the hotspot to the destination. It defines the interaction trigger, actions, and animation settings.

- Destination: The endpoint of the connection. Usually, this is a top-level frame. Only connections using the Scroll to action can be set within the same top-level frame.

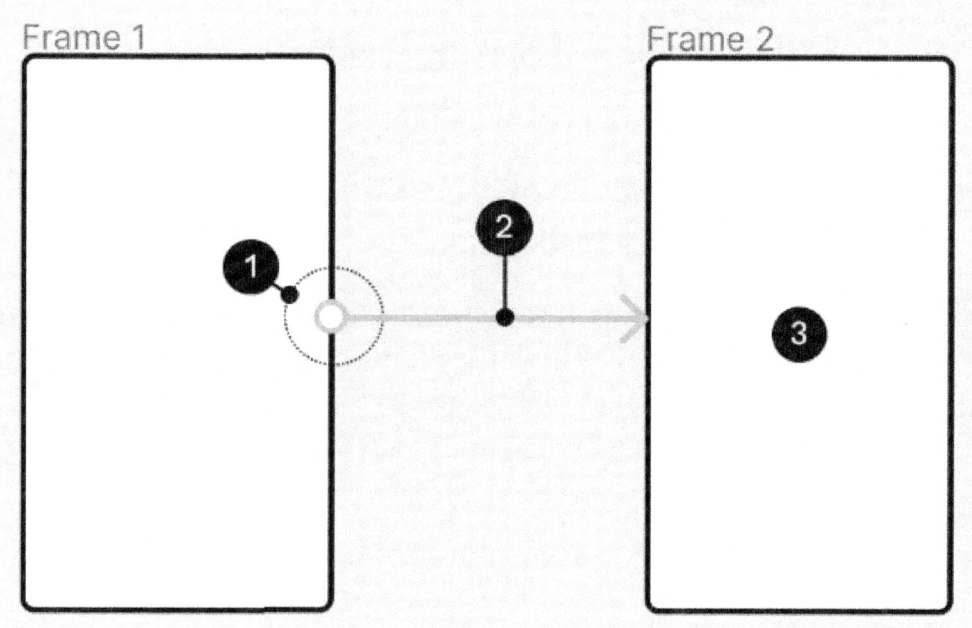

Creating an Interaction:

An interaction is initiated by selecting a hotspot or starting point:

- Switch to Prototype mode by navigating to the Prototype tab in the right sidebar.

- Select a layer or object to serve as the hotspot for the interaction.

Create the interaction by:

- Hovering over the object and dragging the ⊕ plus icon to the destination frame.

- Clicking the '+' plus icon in the Interactions section of the Prototype panel.
- After creating the interaction, use the Interaction details panel to set the trigger, action, animation details, and destination.

Bulk Interaction Creation:

You can create interactions for multiple objects simultaneously:

- Select the starting objects or hotspots where interactions begin. You can select multiple objects by:
    - Holding 'Shift' button and clicking additional objects.
    - Dragging your cursor across the objects.
- Create interactions by hovering over one of the selected objects and dragging the ⊕ plus icon to the destination frame.
- Click the '+' plus icon in the Interactions section of the Prototype panel, and use the Interaction details panel to set the trigger, action, and animation details.

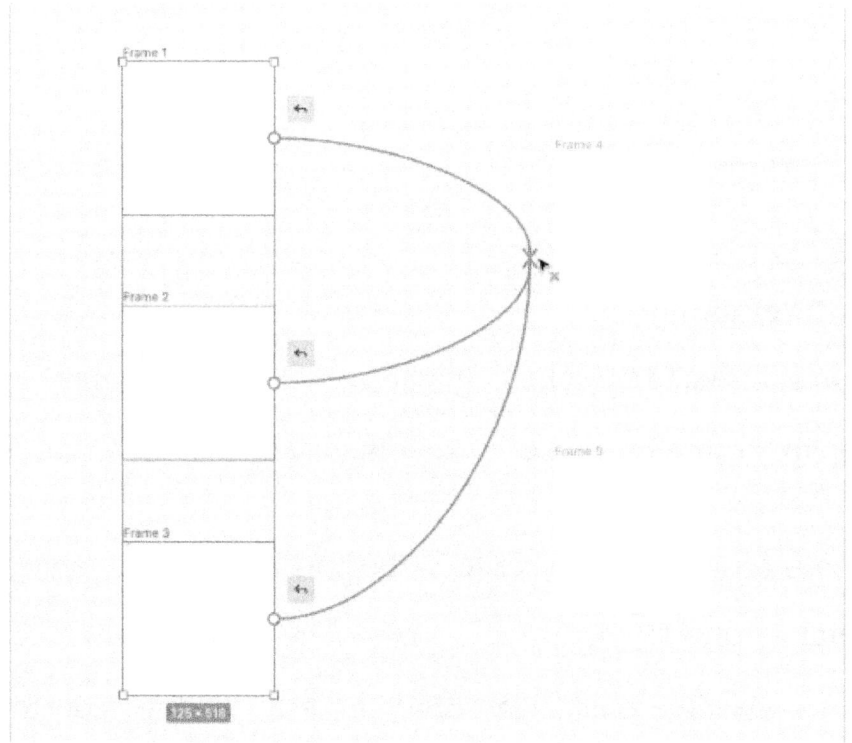

Interaction Details:

After creating an interaction, use the Interaction details modal to configure:

- Trigger: Defines how the interaction starts, such as a mouse click or touch gesture.

- Action: Specifies what happens when the user interacts with the hotspot, like navigating to another frame or opening an overlay.

- Destination: Indicates where the interaction leads, whether to another screen or an overlay.

- Animation Settings: Customize how the prototype transitions between frames, including animation type, direction, easing, and duration.

Managing Interactions:

- Multiple Interactions: A single object can have multiple interactions, each with its own trigger and action.

- Animation Adjustment: Control animation specifics such as type, direction, easing, and duration to refine the transition between frames.

Additional Tools:

- Select Matching Interactions: Identify and select interactions that share the same action and destination across different frames.

- Bulk Destination Editing: Modify the destination of multiple connections simultaneously by selecting and dragging connections or adjusting settings in the Interaction details panel.

- Copy and Paste Interaction Details: Speed up prototyping by copying interaction details from one object and pasting them onto another using keyboard shortcuts.

These tools and techniques enable designers to create detailed and interactive prototypes in Figma, facilitating the visualization and testing of user interactions within digital designs.

Previewing and Sharing Prototypes

To preview and share prototypes in Figma, follow these steps:

Previewing Prototypes:

Enter Prototype Mode:

- Open your Figma file: Click on the "Prototype" tab located at the top right of the interface, or use the shortcut Shift + Command/Ctrl + P to enter Prototype mode.

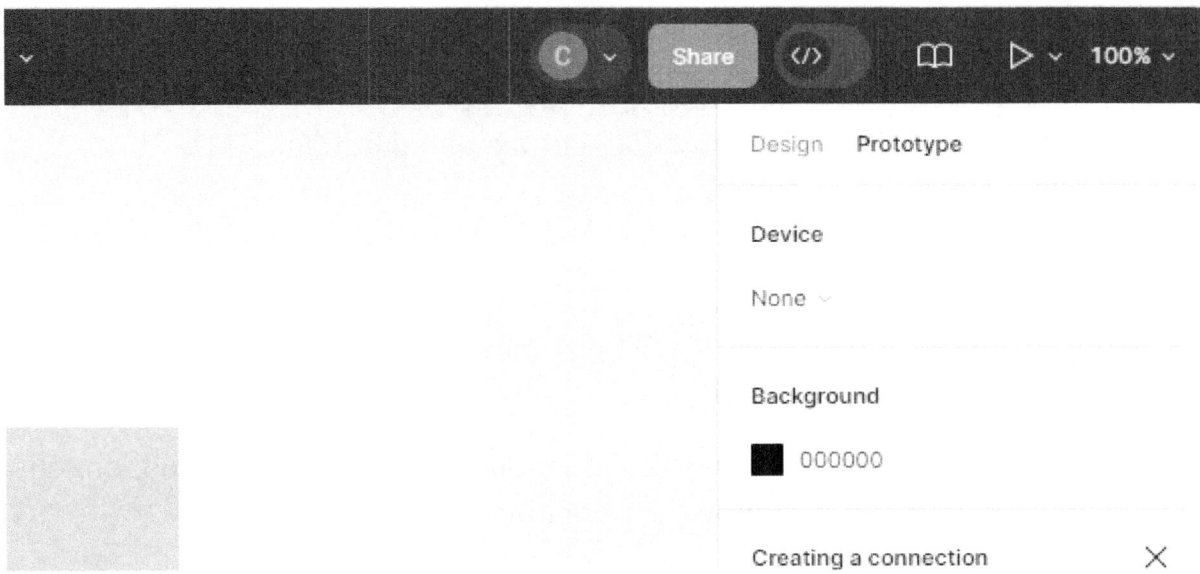

Navigate to the Starting Frame:

- Ensure you're on the frame where you want to begin your prototype.

Activate Preview Mode:

- Click the "Play" button at the top of the Figma interface (next to the Prototype tab) to activate Preview mode.

- Alternatively, use the shortcut Shift + Command/Ctrl + Enter.

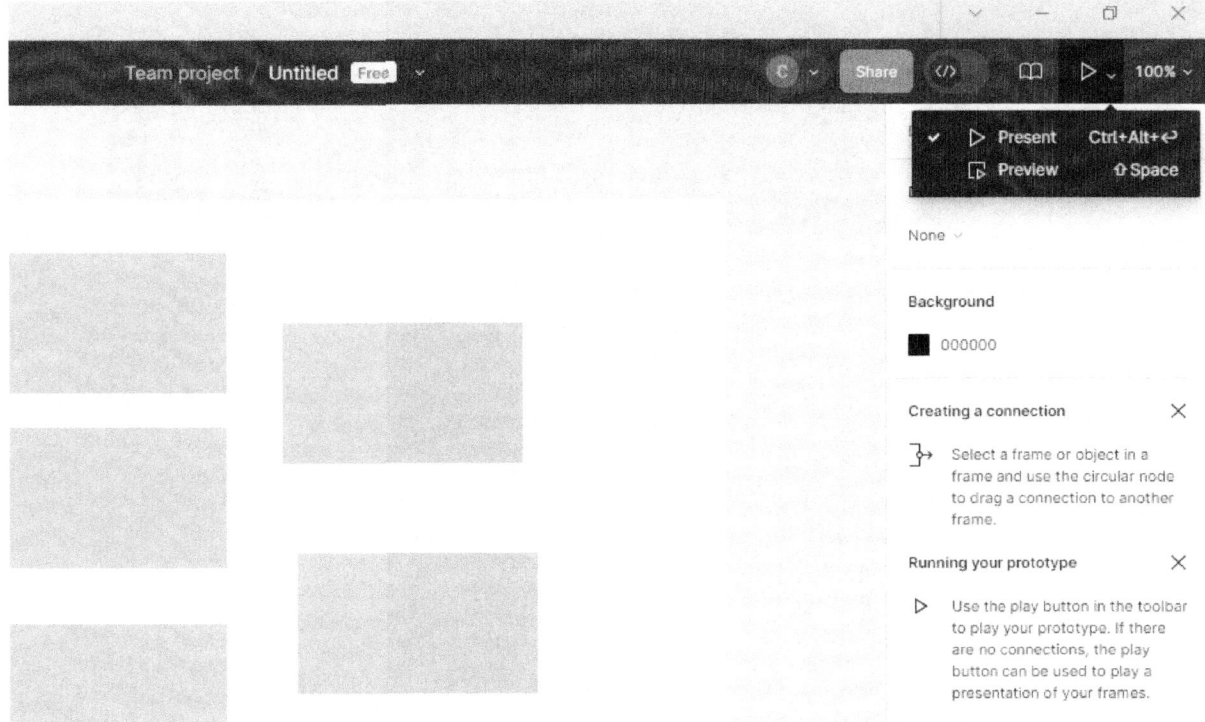

Interact with Your Prototype:

- In Preview mode, interact with your prototype as users would. Click interactive elements to navigate through frames, interact with overlays, and observe animations.

Navigate Between Frames:

- Use defined interactions like clicks or hovers to move between frames and experience the prototype's flow.

Test Responsiveness:

- Resize the preview window to simulate various screen sizes and orientations if your prototype is designed to be responsive.

Sharing Prototypes:

Access Share Mode:

- While in Prototype mode, click on the "Share" tab at the top right of the Figma interface.

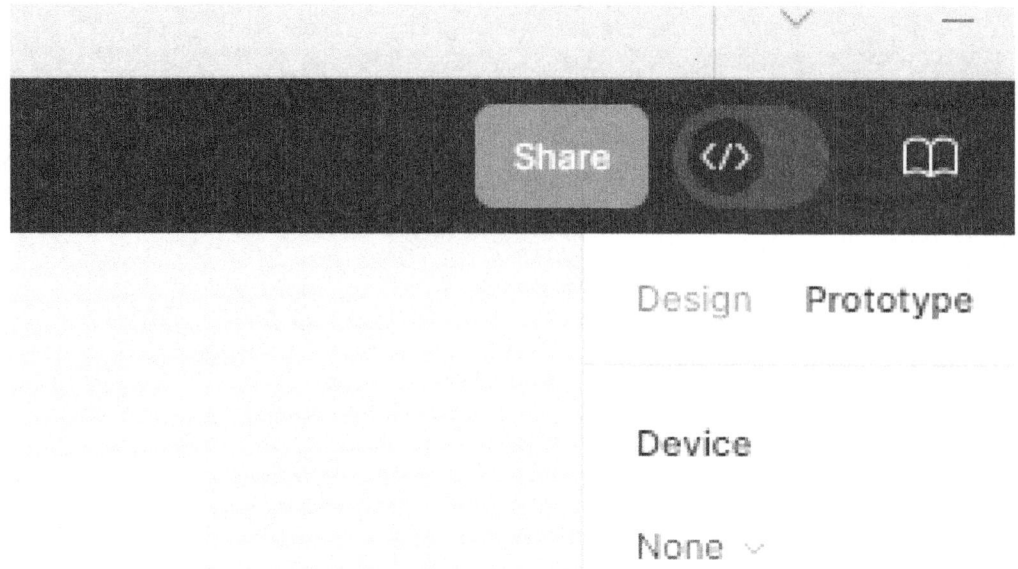

Adjust Share Settings:

Within the Share tab, customize settings as necessary:

- Choose who can access the link (Anyone with the link, People invited to the file, or Only people and groups) under Link Settings.

- Define viewer permissions (comment, view only, edit) under Permissions.

- Optionally, set a password for added security under Password Protection.

- Specify an expiration date for the link if needed under Expiration.

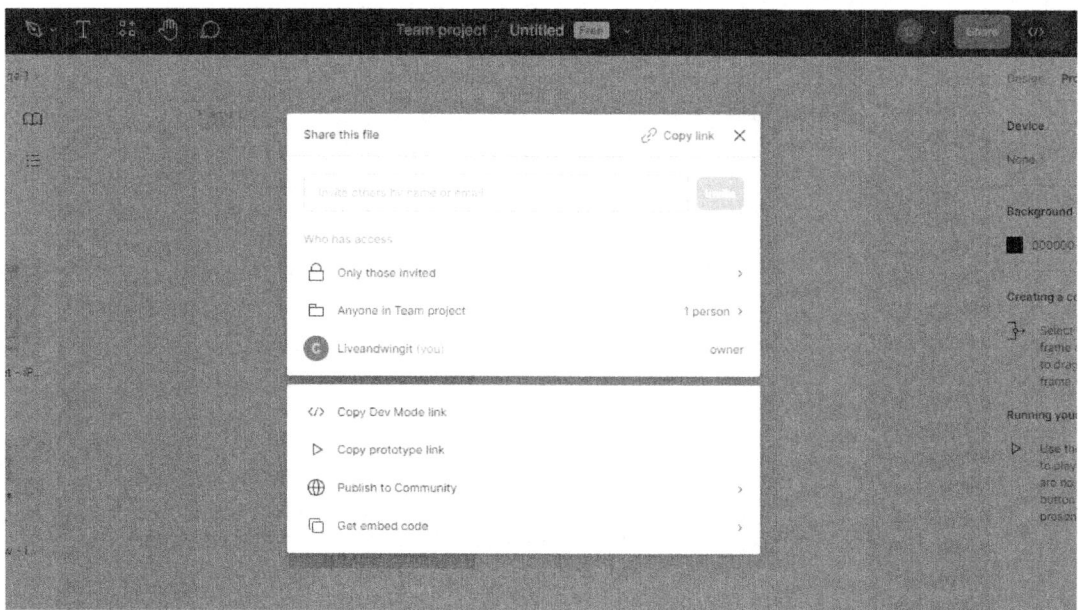

Copy the Shareable Link:

- Click the "Copy link" button to copy the shareable link to your clipboard.

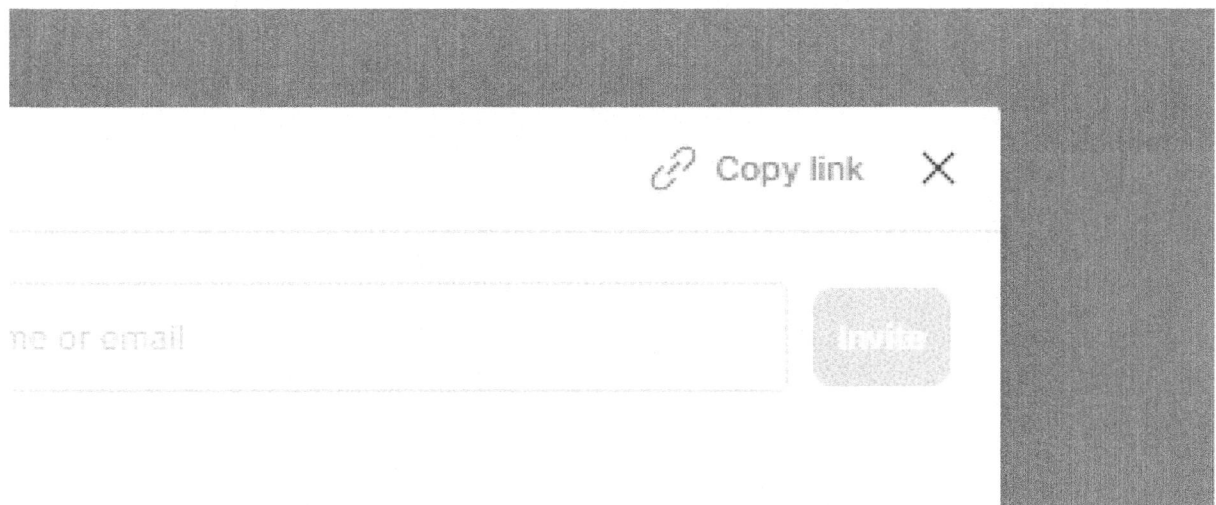

Share the Link:

- Share the copied link with stakeholders, clients, or team members via email, messaging apps, or any preferred communication method.

Viewing the Prototype:

- Recipients can open the shared link in their web browser to view and interact with the prototype in Figma's web view, similar to how it appears in the Figma app.

Following these steps enables efficient previewing and sharing of prototypes in Figma, fostering collaboration and facilitating feedback among project stakeholders.

CHAPTER EIGHT
USER TESTING AND COLLABORATION

Planning and Conducting User Testing Sessions

User testing is a crucial phase in the design process, providing valuable insights into how users interact with your product or prototype. Here's a guide to help you plan and conduct successful user testing sessions for Figma:

Planning Your User Testing Session:

Define Your Objectives:

- Determine what you aim to learn from user testing, whether focusing on usability, user flow, or specific design elements.
- Clear goals help tailor the session and effectively analyze results.

Recruit Participants:

- Identify users who match your target audience in terms of demographics, behavior, and relevant technical skills.
- Aim for a focused group of 5-8 participants to gather comprehensive feedback.

Prepare Your Prototype:

- Ensure your Figma prototype is up-to-date and reflects the latest design iteration.
- Focus on core functionalities and user flows relevant to your testing objectives.
- Prepare clear instructions and an introduction for participants.

Develop a Test Script:

- Create a script outlining tasks participants will complete during the session.
- Include tasks that represent typical user scenarios, allowing flexibility based on user behavior.

Prepare the Testing Environment:

- Choose a quiet, distraction-free location for testing.
- Ensure participants have access to necessary equipment and a smooth interaction with your Figma prototype.
- Consider recording sessions with participant consent for later analysis.

Conducting the User Testing Session:

Welcome and Introduction:

- Welcome participants and create a comfortable environment.
- Explain the session's purpose and what insights you hope to gather.
- Obtain consent for recording (if applicable).

Warm-Up Tasks:

- Start with simple tasks to familiarize participants with the prototype and testing process.

Main Testing Phase:

- Guide participants through predefined tasks in your script.
- Observe their interactions, thought processes, and any challenges they encounter.
- Encourage participants to vocalize their thoughts ("think aloud") while navigating the prototype.

Wrap-Up and Feedback:

- Thank participants for their time and feedback.
- Summarize key observations and invite final questions.
- Optionally, offer incentives for participation.

Analyzing and Documenting Findings:

Review Recordings and Notes:

- Analyze session recordings and notes to identify recurring themes and user pain points.
- Pay attention to verbal cues and non-verbal reactions.

Identify Improvement Opportunities:

- Based on user feedback and observations, pinpoint areas where the design can be enhanced.
- Focus on usability issues, confusing elements, or tasks where users encountered difficulties.

Prioritize Improvements:

- Prioritize design changes based on their impact and severity on user experience.

Document Your Findings:

- Create a comprehensive report summarizing key observations, user feedback, and proposed improvements.
- Use this report to guide future design iterations and ensure valuable insights are integrated.

Additional Tips:

Maintain Objectivity:

- Approach user testing with openness to learn from user behavior, avoiding defensiveness about design choices.

Stay Focused:

- While user feedback is valuable, prioritize improvements aligned with your initial testing goals.

Iterate and Refine:

- Use user testing insights to iteratively improve your design in Figma.

- Conduct follow-up sessions as needed to validate design changes and ensure usability enhancements.

Following these steps and best practices enables effective user testing sessions in Figma, leveraging valuable feedback to create user-centric designs that are intuitive and meet the needs of your target audience. your productivity and creativity across various tasks.

Using Figma for User Feedback and Iteration

Figma's interactive prototyping capabilities make it a robust tool for collecting user feedback and continuously refining your designs. Here's how to maximize Figma throughout your design process to enhance user experiences:

Creating Interactive Prototypes in Figma:

- Starting Simple, Building Up: Avoid overwhelming users with complex animations. Begin by establishing foundational elements such as buttons, links, and forms. Define different states (default, hover, active) to provide visual feedback. Use Figma's prototyping features to connect frames and simulate user navigation.

- Enhancing Clarity with Microinteractions: Improve user experience by incorporating subtle animations or microinteractions. Consider integrating loading spinners, success animations, or error indicators for a more polished interface.

Gathering User Feedback:

- Harnessing the Power of Sharing: Once you've developed a functional prototype, utilize Figma's sharing capabilities. Generate a shareable link and distribute it among your target audience, stakeholders, or design team

- Providing Context: Always accompany your prototype with clear explanations of its design goals, target user, and specific areas where feedback is sought.

- Utilizing Figma's Feedback Tools: Encourage viewers to leave comments directly on the prototype using Figma's commenting features. This enables precise feedback on elements or interactions that require improvement.

Iteration and Refinement:

- Analyzing Feedback: Carefully review and analyze the feedback received on your prototype. Identify recurring themes and pinpoint areas that users found challenging or confusing.

- Prioritizing Improvements: Based on feedback insights, prioritize enhancements, focusing first on critical usability issues that impact user experience.

- Refining and Iterating: Utilize Figma's editing tools to iterate on your design. Refine interactions, animations, and user flows based on the feedback gathered, aiming for continuous improvement.

Additional Tips:

- Conducting Usability Testing: Consider organizing formal usability testing sessions within Figma, involving a small group of users to observe their interactions and identify nuanced usability issues.

- Testing Across Devices: Use Figma's device preview mode to ensure your prototype functions seamlessly across various screen sizes, including desktops, tablets, and mobile phones.

- Maintaining a Feedback Loop: Integrate continuous feedback collection and iteration throughout your design process to iteratively enhance the user experience.

Benefits of Using Figma for User Feedback and Iteration:

- Early Issue Identification: By gathering user feedback early in the design process, you can save time and effort compared to addressing issues later in development.

- Data-Driven Design Decisions: User feedback offers valuable insights that inform design decisions, ensuring your design meets user needs and expectations effectively.

- Improved User Experience: Through iterative refinement based on user feedback, you can create intuitive and visually appealing user experiences.

Collaboration Tools and Features in Figma

Figma excels not only in its prototyping capabilities but also in its comprehensive suite of collaboration tools and features. These tools empower design teams to collaborate seamlessly throughout the design process, ensuring cohesion and efficiency.

Here's an overview of Figma's key collaboration features:

- Real-Time Collaboration: Figma allows multiple team members to work simultaneously on the same project in real-time. Changes are visible instantly to all participants, promoting better communication and accelerating iteration cycles.

- Project Sharing and Access Control: Easily manage access to projects by granting different permissions—viewing, commenting, or editing—to team members based on their roles. This ensures secure and collaborative design sessions.

- Centralized File Storage: All design files are stored in the cloud, ensuring that team members always access the latest version. This centralized storage eliminates version control issues and keeps the team synchronized.

- Version History and Branching: Track changes with Figma's version history, allowing you to revert to previous iterations as needed. Branching enables creating separate design explorations without affecting the main project file.

- Built-in Design Handoff: Facilitate smooth handoff to developers by generating code snippets, exporting assets in various formats, and including design specs directly within Figma. This ensures clear communication between design and development teams.

- Commenting and Feedback: Foster constructive feedback with Figma's commenting system, where team members can leave comments directly on specific design elements. This promotes focused discussions and efficient issue resolution.

- Team Libraries and Components: Establish centralized repositories of reusable design elements such as buttons, icons, and color palettes. This promotes design consistency across projects and saves time by avoiding redundant work.

- Integrations: Extend Figma's functionality by integrating it with popular tools like Slack, Jira, and Asana. This integration streamlines workflow and communication within the design ecosystem.

Benefits of Figma's Collaboration Features:

- Improved Communication: Real-time collaboration and centralized communication tools enhance transparency and facilitate better communication within design teams.

- Faster Iteration Cycles: Immediate feedback and simultaneous editing capabilities enable faster iteration and refinement of designs.

- Reduced Errors and Confusion: Centralized file storage and version control minimize confusion caused by outdated or misplaced design files, leading to more efficient workflows.

- Unified Design Language: Team libraries and component systems ensure consistency in design elements across projects, maintaining a cohesive brand identity.

- Streamlined Workflow: Integrations with external tools reduce context switching and streamline workflows, improving overall efficiency in design processes.

By leveraging Figma's robust collaboration features, design teams can work together effectively, fostering a collaborative environment that enhances productivity and leads to outstanding design outcomes.

CHAPTER NINE
PLUGINS AND INTEGRATION TO ENHANCE FIGMA

Exploring Figma Plugin Ecosystem

Figma distinguishes itself in the realm of design tools by enabling collaborative and efficient creation of striking interfaces. A standout aspect of Figma is its robust plugin ecosystem, which greatly extends the platform's inherent capabilities. Dive into the realm of Figma plugins and their potential to improve design workflows and unlock new creative opportunities.

Understanding Figma Plugins:

Figma plugins are third-party tools developed by the community to expand and enhance the functionality of the Figma platform. These plugins operate like miniature applications within Figma, giving designers access to a wide range of features and integrations. They automate repetitive tasks, integrate with external services, and enhance design tools, offering numerous advantages that streamline workflows and enhance design quality.

Here are key plugins that work well with Figma:

- Illustrations: Provides a library of pre-designed graphics to effortlessly enhance visual designs.

- ProtoPie: Enables exporting interactive, high-fidelity prototypes directly from Figma.

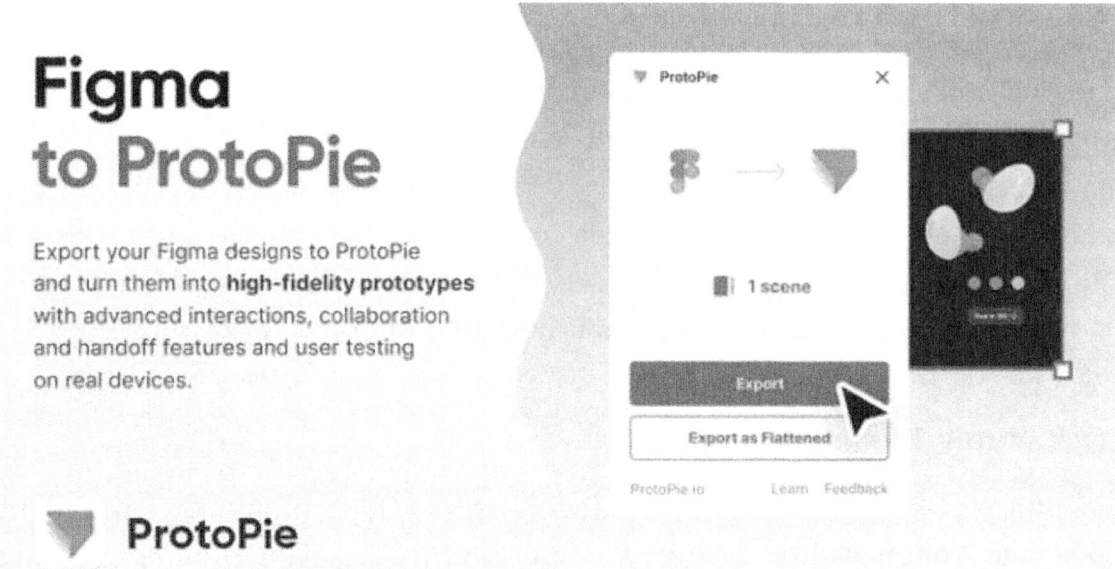

- Pitchdeck Presentation Studio: Facilitates easy creation of animated presentations within Figma, exportable to various formats.

- Autoflow: Simplifies creation of user flows, diagrams, and graphics in hand-drawn or minimalist styles.

- UIHUT: Grants access to an extensive library of UI kits, web templates, illustrations, 3D assets, and icons for designers and teams.

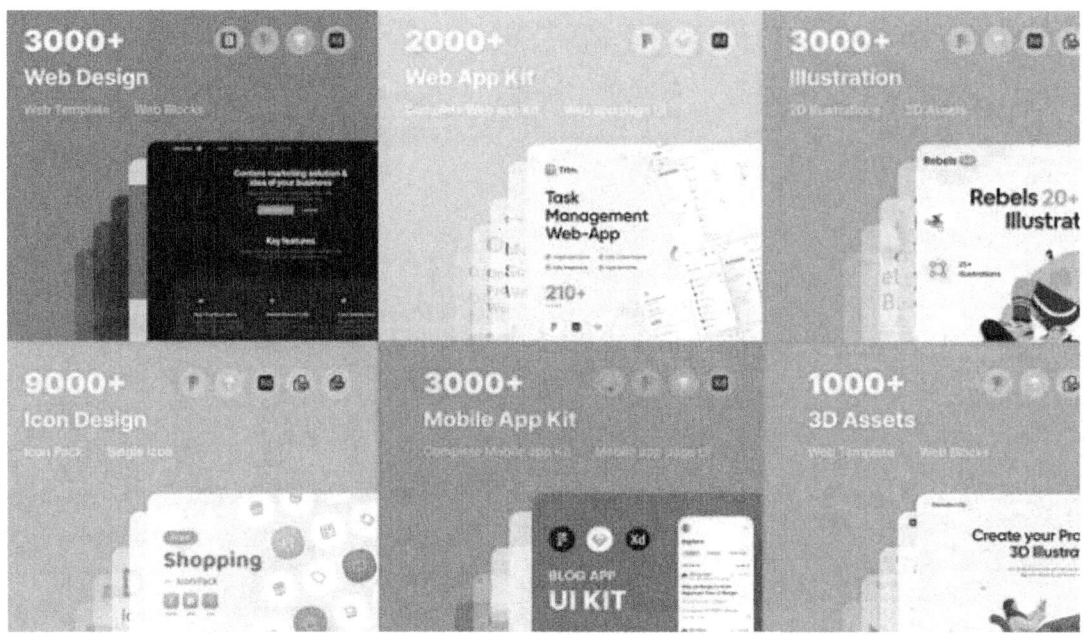

- Blush: Generates customizable illustrations, facilitating unique visual aesthetics for designs.

- Tokens Studio: Enables the use of design tokens for consistent styling across documents in Figma.

- ColorWell: Provides intuitive color mixing, palette creation, and application within Figma designs.

- SmoothShadow: Creates layered and smooth shadows to enhance design depth.

- Image Tracer: Converts images into scalable vector layers and offers versatile styling options.

- IconScout: Provides access to millions of customizable SVGs, vector icons, and illustrations.

- Palette: Automatically generates color palettes from design elements or images used in Figma projects.

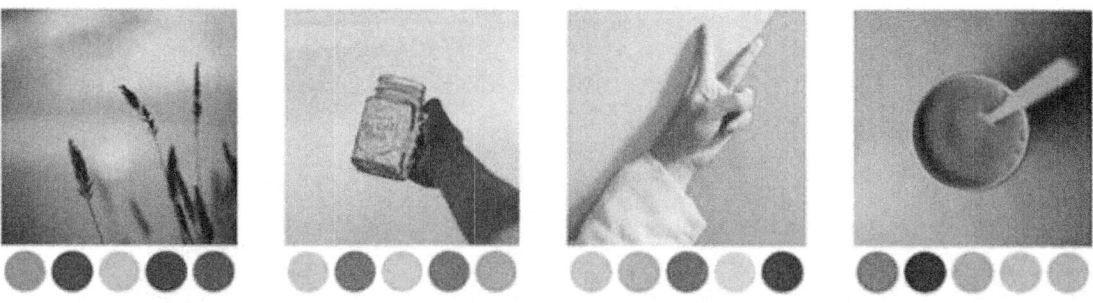

Figma plugins are indispensable for designers looking to streamline workflows, expand creative capabilities, and innovate in design. Leveraging plugins automates tasks, enhances collaboration, ensures design consistency, and encourages creative exploration. Whether you're new to Figma or an experienced designer, exploring plugins opens new horizons for advancing design practices and achieving outstanding results.

Using Plugin to Supercharge Your Design Workflow

Figma is a potent design tool, but its capabilities can expand significantly with plugins. These third-party add-ons provide a wide range of functionalities, allowing you to tailor Figma to your specific design requirements and streamline your workflow.

Here's a glimpse into the diverse world of Figma plugins:

- Prototyping & Interaction Design: Enhance your prototypes using advanced animation tools, microinteraction libraries, and plugins with conditional logic. Imagine crafting prototypes featuring intricate user flows and state-based interactions that emulate real-world app behavior.

- Data Design & Visualization: Convert static data into compelling visuals. Plugins can connect Figma to external data sources, enabling you to populate charts, graphs, and interfaces with real-time data. This is ideal for developing interactive dashboards or data-driven prototypes.

- Content Creation & Design Assets: Generate placeholder text, create realistic mockups with stock photos, or explore icon libraries for efficient design processes. These plugins save time and effort in sourcing content for your designs.

- Accessibility & Usability: Ensure your designs are inclusive and user-friendly. Plugins can identify potential accessibility issues, check color contrast ratios, or generate alternative text descriptions for images.

- Design System Management: Maintain consistency across your design system with plugin tools. These tools assist in managing design tokens (colors, fonts, spacing), producing component documentation, and ensuring consistent application of your design language.

- Workflow Optimization & Productivity: Enhance design efficiency with plugins that automate repetitive tasks, organize design files, or integrate Figma with other tools. Imagine batch exporting assets, decluttering files, or collaborating seamlessly with developers directly within Figma.

Keep in Mind: While plugins offer diverse features, avoid cluttering your Figma workspace. Select plugins that seamlessly integrate with your workflow and target specific challenges in your design process.

Integrating Figma with Other Design and Development Tools

Integrating Figma with a variety of design and development tools expands its functionality and enhances collaborative workflows. Here's an exploration of how Figma integrates with different tools to support various aspects of the design process:

Streamlining Developer Handoff: Tools like Zeplin, Avocode, or Inspect by InVision simplify the transition from design to development. They extract code snippets, CSS styles, and measurements directly from Figma designs, ensuring precise implementation and minimizing communication gaps between designers and developers.

Enhancing Version Control: Integrate Figma seamlessly with version control systems such as GitHub, GitLab, or Bitbucket using plugins or native integrations. This integration enables teams to monitor changes, collaborate on design revisions, and maintain a centralized repository for design files alongside code repositories.

Improving Project Management: Connect Figma with project management platforms like Jira, Asana, Trello, or Monday.com. By syncing tasks, milestones, and design updates, teams streamline project coordination, improve visibility, and ensure alignment between design progress and overall project timelines.

Facilitating Communication: Integrate Figma with communication tools such as Slack or Microsoft Teams to enhance team collaboration. These integrations enable real-time notifications, threaded discussions, and direct file sharing within chat channels, promoting efficient feedback loops and reducing workflow interruptions.

Managing Design Systems: Use tools like Abstract or Zeroheight alongside Figma to manage design systems and component libraries. These integrations support consistent design across projects, facilitate global updates to design assets, and ensure adherence to brand guidelines across the board.

Advanced Prototyping and Animation: Integrate Figma with prototyping and animation tools like Principle or ProtoPie for sophisticated interactions and animations. These integrations empower designers to create high-fidelity prototypes with intricate transitions and interactions, enhancing user experience testing and validation.

Secure Cloud Storage: Connect Figma with cloud storage platforms such as Google Drive, Dropbox, or Box for secure storage and management of design files. These integrations ensure accessibility, version control, and backup of Figma projects, promoting collaboration across distributed teams and safeguarding against data loss.

Efficient Collaboration Platforms: Platforms like Marvel or UXPin integrate seamlessly with Figma to streamline design collaboration, user testing, and feedback collection. These integrations facilitate the smooth transfer of Figma prototypes to testing environments and stakeholder reviews, supporting iterative design processes and improving overall design outcomes.

Integrating Figma with these diverse tools and platforms will help designers and teams optimize productivity, streamline workflows, and foster collaboration throughout the design and development lifecycle. These integrations enable seamless communication, efficient project management, and elevated design quality, ultimately leading to improved outcomes and user experiences.

CHAPTER TEN
DESIGN HANDOFF AND DEVELOPMENT

Preparing Design Assets for Developers

The connection between impressive design and functional development hinges on well-prepared and transparent design assets. As a designer, ensuring that developers receive organized and easily understandable assets facilitates a seamless handoff and mitigates obstacles during development. Here's a guide to assist you in preparing your design assets for developers:

Organize Your Assets:

- Structured Folders: Maintain a logical folder structure within your design tool (like Figma). Group assets such as icons, illustrations, and UI elements into clearly labeled folders for straightforward navigation by developers.

- Naming Conventions: Implement consistent and descriptive naming conventions for your assets. Use names that explicitly indicate the element's purpose and role (e.g., "btn-primary.svg", "hero-banner-background.jpg"). Avoid ambiguous or abbreviated names that could cause confusion.

Export Assets in Suitable Formats:

- Consider Development Requirements: Select file formats that align with the tools and technologies used in development. Common formats include SVG for scalable graphics, PNG for images requiring transparency, and JPG for photographic content.

- Export Settings: Use your design tool's export settings to manage file quality and size effectively. Aim for a balance between preserving visual fidelity and ensuring efficient integration into development workflows.

Prepare Sliced Assets (if applicable):

- Complex Layouts: For intricate designs with multiple grouped elements (e.g., product card components), consider exporting sliced assets as individual PNGs. This simplifies implementation, particularly in web development using CSS frameworks.

- Alternative Approaches: In some cases, providing the original design file (e.g., Figma) with clear organization and naming conventions may suffice for developers to extract necessary assets.

Include Design Specifications and Annotations:

- Clarity in Documentation: Accompany your assets with precise documentation. Include specifications detailing element dimensions, spacing, colors, fonts, and any specific implementation instructions. Annotations within your design tool can also highlight critical elements or functionalities.

- Utilize Style Guides: If available, incorporate a comprehensive style guide that defines your design system. This acts as a centralized reference for developers regarding all design elements and their intended usage.

Consider Version Control (Optional):

- Tracking Changes: For larger projects or those undergoing frequent design iterations, contemplate utilizing version control systems like Git. This enables developers to track modifications made to design assets, facilitating easier reference and consistency checks.

Additional Tips:

- Developer-Oriented Tools: Leverage built-in developer handoff features in tools like Figma, offering functionalities such as code snippet generation and design inspection. These tools streamline the handoff process and furnish developers with pertinent information directly from the design environment.

- Effective Communication: Maintain open lines of communication with developers throughout the design phase. Discuss specific requirements and potential challenges early on to ensure a smooth and efficient handoff.

- Testing and Iteration: Be prepared to iterate on design assets based on feedback from developers. This collaborative approach ensures that the final product aligns with both the initial design vision and practical development considerations.

Using Figma for Developer Specifications and Style Guides

Figma plays a crucial role in translating design concepts into actionable developer specifications and comprehensive style guides, fostering efficient collaboration between design and development teams to ensure clarity and consistency throughout the project lifecycle. Below, we explore how Figma can effectively be utilized for these purposes:

Creating Developer Specifications:

- Documentation of Components: Use Figma to meticulously document design components, detailing dimensions, spacing, typography, color codes, and interactive states. This detailed documentation assists developers in accurately implementing design elements.

- Inspection Tools: Utilize Figma's inspection tools to extract CSS attributes, font styles, and precise measurements directly from designs. This feature enables developers to access essential details without unnecessary communication loops.

Developing Comprehensive Style Guides:

- Centralized Design System: Establish a centralized repository within Figma for design system components. Organize styles, symbols, and reusable elements to maintain consistency across projects and iterations.

- Interactive Prototypes: Employ Figma to create interactive prototypes that demonstrate design principles and user interactions. These prototypes serve as live examples within your style guide, providing practical insights into design intentions for developers.

Facilitating Collaboration:

- Real-time Updates: Take advantage of Figma's real-time collaboration features to ensure developers have access to the latest design iterations and updates. This minimizes discrepancies and enhances team alignment throughout the design and development phases.

- Feedback Loops: Use Figma's commenting and annotation features to facilitate constructive feedback exchanges between designers and developers. This interactive feedback loop supports iterative improvements and efficiently resolves design implementation queries.

Integrating with Development Workflows:

- Handoff Tools: Utilize Figma's integration with developer handoff platforms such as Zeplin or Avocode. These integrations streamline the handoff process by automatically generating code snippets, CSS styles, and exporting assets, ensuring smooth translation of design specifications into functional code.

Ensuring Accessibility and Usability:

- Accessibility Checks: Use Figma's plugins and design tools to conduct accessibility audits. Verify color contrast ratios, text readability, and screen reader compatibility to ensure inclusive design practices.

By leveraging Figma for developer specifications and style guides, teams can cultivate a collaborative environment, streamline workflows, and maintain design integrity across projects. This integration empowers both designers and developers to deliver cohesive, user-centric digital experiences efficiently.

Collaboration Between Designers and Developers

Collaboration between designers and developers plays a pivotal role in transforming design concepts into functional digital experiences. Effective teamwork ensures alignment throughout the project lifecycle. We explore methods to boost collaboration between designers and developers below:

Promoting Clear Communication Channels:

- Encourage transparent communication channels between designers and developers to discuss design objectives, technical limitations, and implementation tactics. Regular meetings and collaborative tools such as Slack or Microsoft Teams facilitate ongoing discussions.

Establishing a Unified Vision of Design Intent:

- Ensure designers clearly articulate design intentions, supported by visual references and interactive prototypes crafted in tools like Figma. This aids developers in comprehending user experience objectives and making well-informed implementation decisions.

Enabling Iterative Feedback Mechanisms:

- Create iterative feedback loops where developers offer insights on design feasibility and usability early in the process. Designers can iteratively integrate feedback, ensuring alignment with technical specifications.

Utilizing Documentation and Annotations:

- Employ tools like Figma to document design choices, annotations, and specifications directly within design files. This centralizes information, minimizes ambiguity, and serves as a reference for both designers and developers.

Facilitating Collaborative Design Systems:

- Maintain a shared design system in platforms like Figma, enabling designers and developers to access and contribute to a repository of reusable components, styles, and guidelines. This fosters consistency and efficiency across projects.

Integrating Design and Development Workflows:

- Integrate design and development workflows by leveraging tools such as Zeplin, Avocode, or InVision Inspect. These tools facilitate seamless transfer of design assets, generating code snippets and specifications directly from design files to streamline implementation.

Encouraging Cross-functional Training and Awareness:

- Promote cross-functional understanding by equipping developers with foundational design principles and providing designers with essential knowledge of development constraints. This cultivates empathy, collaboration, and effective problem-solving.

Conducting Regular Reviews and Demonstrations:

- Host routine design reviews and demonstrations where designers showcase prototypes and designs to developers. This interactive process encourages feedback, validates design decisions, and ensures alignment with project objectives.

By adopting these strategies, teams can nurture a collaborative environment between designers and developers, enhancing communication, optimizing workflows, and ultimately delivering cohesive, user-centric digital products efficiently.

CHAPTER ELEVEN
ADVANCED CUSTOMIZATION AND WORKFLOWS

Customizing Your Figma Workspace

Customizing your Figma workspace allows you to adapt the environment to meet your specific design requirements and preferences. Here's how you can personalize and optimize your Figma workspace:

Creating Custom Workspaces:

- Set up personalized workspaces in Figma by arranging panels, tools, and views according to your workflow. Customize the layout to prioritize frequently used features and streamline access to essential tools.

Tailoring Keyboard Shortcuts:

- Personalize keyboard shortcuts within Figma to streamline common tasks and workflows. Assign shortcuts to frequently used tools, commands, or menu options to enhance efficiency and minimize manual navigation.

Organizing and Utilizing Plugins:

- Incorporate plugins into your Figma setup to expand functionality. Explore and install plugins that cater to your unique design needs, organizing them within Figma for convenient access and effective utilization.

Adapting Color Themes and UI Preferences:

- Adjust color themes and UI preferences in Figma to align with your visual style and improve usability. Customize interface elements such as canvas background colors, grid settings, and theme accents to create a workspace that suits your aesthetic preferences.

Managing Libraries and Assets:

- Utilize Figma libraries to manage and structure design assets, components, and styles across projects. Establish and maintain libraries containing reusable elements to ensure consistency and efficiency in your design workflows.

Harnessing Team Collaboration Tools:

- Take advantage of Figma's collaboration features to facilitate team communication and coordination. Set permissions, share designs, and collaborate in real-time with teammates to streamline project workflows and feedback processes.

Integrating External Tools and Services:

- Integrate external tools and services with Figma to enhance functionality and workflow capabilities. Connect Figma with developer handoff platforms, version control systems, or prototyping tools to streamline the transition from design to development.

Exploring New Features and Enhancements:

- Stay updated on the latest Figma features and enhancements. Regularly explore and adopt new functionalities that enhance productivity, optimize workflows, and support evolving design practices.

By customizing your Figma workspace effectively, you can create a tailored environment that enhances your design process, boosts productivity, and fosters seamless collaboration with team members and external collaborators.

Keyboard Shortcuts

Mastering keyboard shortcuts in Figma can greatly improve your efficiency and streamline your design workflow. Here's a guide to help you become proficient in using keyboard shortcuts in Figma:

Essential Shortcuts:

Selection and Tools:

- V: Move tool
- A: Frame tool
- T: Text tool
- P: Pen tool
- R: Rectangle tool
- L: Line tool

Basic Actions:

- Cmd/Ctrl + C: Copy
- Cmd/Ctrl + V: Paste
- Cmd/Ctrl + X: Cut
- Cmd/Ctrl + Z: Undo
- Cmd/Ctrl + Shift + Z: Redo
- Cmd/Ctrl + D: Duplicate

Navigating the Canvas:

Zooming:

- Cmd/Ctrl + +/-: Zoom in/out
- Cmd/Ctrl + 0: Fit to screen
- Cmd/Ctrl + 1: 100% zoom

Panning and Moving:

- Spacebar + Drag: Pan the canvas
- Cmd/Ctrl + Drag: Select and move objects

Managing Layers and Objects:

Layer Ordering:

- Cmd/Ctrl +]: Bring forward
- Cmd/Ctrl + [: Send backward
- Cmd/Ctrl + Shift +]: Bring to front
- Cmd/Ctrl + Shift + [: Send to back

Grouping:

- Cmd/Ctrl + G: Group selected objects
- Cmd/Ctrl + Shift + G: Ungroup objects

Aligning and Distributing:

- Cmd/Ctrl + Option + A: Align horizontally
- Cmd/Ctrl + Option + D: Distribute horizontally
- Cmd/Ctrl + Option + H: Align vertically
- Cmd/Ctrl + Option + V: Distribute vertically

Working with Text:

Text Editing:

- Cmd/Ctrl + B: Bold
- Cmd/Ctrl + I: Italic
- Cmd/Ctrl + U: Underline

Advanced Shortcuts:

Guides and Grids:

- Cmd/Ctrl + R: Show/hide rulers
- Cmd/Ctrl + ;: Show/hide guides
- Cmd/Ctrl + /: Show/hide layout grid

Quick Actions:

- Cmd/Ctrl + /: Open quick actions menu
- Cmd/Ctrl + .: Toggle UI visibility

Customizing Shortcuts:

- Figma allows you to customize your shortcuts to better suit your workflow. Go to Preferences > Keyboard Shortcuts to modify existing shortcuts or create new ones that match your specific needs.

Tips for Mastering Shortcuts:

- Start Small: Begin by learning the shortcuts for the tools and actions you use most frequently.
- Practice Regularly: Use shortcuts consistently to build muscle memory.
- Use Cheat Sheets: Keep a list of commonly used shortcuts nearby until you've memorized them.
- Watch Tutorials: Many online resources and videos can help you learn and practice shortcuts in context.

Advanced Tips and Tricks for Expert Figma Users

As you grow more adept with Figma, diving into its advanced features and techniques can significantly boost your productivity and creativity. Here are some expert tips to elevate your Figma skills:

Component Overrides and Variants:

Component Overrides:

- Modify individual instances of components by changing text, colors, images, and other properties without altering the original component. This allows for unique variations while maintaining consistency.

Variants:

- Create multiple states or versions of a component within a single main component, ideal for elements like buttons with different states (e.g., hover, active, disabled).

Mastering Auto Layout:

Nested Auto Layout:

- Combine multiple Auto Layout frames to design complex, responsive layouts. Nesting these frames allows elements to resize and align dynamically based on content changes.

Padding and Spacing:

- Precisely control layout by adjusting padding and spacing settings. Set individual padding values for top, bottom, left, and right to fine-tune your design.

Advanced Prototyping:

Interactive Components:

- Develop interactive components with hover, click, and transition states for more realistic and dynamic prototypes, enhancing user testing.

Prototype Overlays:

- Implement overlays to create pop-ups, modals, and tooltips. Overlays can be triggered by interactions and positioned relative to the main frame.

Efficient Design Systems Management:

Shared Libraries:

- Use Figma's Team Library feature to share and manage design assets across projects. Centralize components, styles, and assets to maintain consistency.

Design Tokens:

- Apply design tokens to ensure consistent use of colors, typography, spacing, and other properties across different platforms and devices.

Leveraging Plugins for Advanced Functionality:

Content Reel:

- Quickly populate designs with realistic text, images, and user data using the Content Reel plugin, making mockups and prototypes more lifelike.

Stark:

- Conduct accessibility checks with the Stark plugin to ensure your designs meet standards by verifying color contrast, generating alt text, and simulating color blindness.

Optimizing Performance:

Component Instances:

- Use component instances instead of duplicating elements to reduce file size and improve performance, ensuring consistency.

Optimize Images:

- Compress and optimize images before importing them into Figma to reduce file size and improve loading times.

Advanced Keyboard Shortcuts and Customization:

Custom Shortcuts:

- Tailor keyboard shortcuts to your workflow by adjusting settings in Preferences > Keyboard Shortcuts.

Nested Frames Navigation:

- Quickly navigate nested frames and components using shortcuts like Cmd/Ctrl + Enter for efficient editing.

Collaborative Techniques:

Design Critiques:

- Utilize Figma's commenting feature for collaborative design critiques. Encourage team members to leave feedback directly on designs, fostering iterative improvements.

Real-time Collaboration:

- Leverage Figma's real-time collaboration features to work simultaneously with team members on the same file, enabling immediate feedback and faster iterations.

Mastering these advanced tips and tricks can help you unlock Figma's full potential, making your design process more efficient, collaborative, and creatively rewarding.

CHAPTER TWELVE
TROUBLESHOOTING AND RESOURCES

Common Issues and Solutions

Performance Slowdowns:

Issue: Figma may slow down with large files or intricate designs.

Solution:

- Optimize Assets: Compress and optimize images before importing.
- Use Component Instances: Replace duplicated elements with component instances to reduce file size.
- Clean Up Layers: Eliminate unnecessary layers and elements to streamline design files.

Syncing and Collaboration Delays:

Issue: Real-time collaboration and syncing might lag or fail.

Solution:

- Check Internet Connection: Ensure a stable and fast internet connection.
- Clear Browser Cache: Clear your browser cache and cookies if using Figma on the web.
- Update Figma: Use the latest version of Figma, as updates often improve performance and fix bugs.

Missing Fonts:

Issue: Fonts used in a design are missing, affecting text rendering.

Solution:

- Install Fonts: Ensure all required fonts are installed on your computer.
- Use Google Fonts: Opt for Google Fonts or other web-safe fonts to avoid compatibility issues.
- Font Manager: Use Figma's Font Manager to identify and replace missing fonts.

Export Quality Issues:

Issue: Exported assets appear blurry or low quality.

Solution:

- Check Export Settings: Ensure assets are exported at the correct resolution and format.

- Use SVG for Vectors: For vector graphics, use the SVG format to maintain scalability and quality.

- Pixel Grid: Align elements to the pixel grid to avoid anti-aliasing issues and ensure sharp edges.

Component Overrides Not Working:

Issue: Component overrides do not apply correctly or revert unexpectedly.

Solution:

- Check Overrides: Ensure overrides are applied to the correct component instances.

- Update Components: Update the main component if overrides are not reflecting properly.

- Detach Instances: If overrides are problematic, consider detaching the instance and making manual adjustments.

Auto Layout Issues:

Issue: Elements in Auto Layout frames do not align or resize as expected.

Solution:

- Review Settings: Check Auto Layout settings for padding, spacing, and alignment.

- Nested Frames: Ensure nested Auto Layout frames are configured correctly to work together.

- Content Resize: Adjust content resize settings to 'Fill Container' or 'Hug Contents' as needed.

Prototyping Bugs:

Issue: Prototypes do not behave as intended, with interactions not working correctly.

Solution:

- Check Links: Verify all prototype links and interactions are set up correctly.
- Reset Prototype: Restart the prototype to see if the issue persists.
- Simplify Interactions: Break down complex interactions into simpler steps to isolate the issue.

Version Control Problems:

Issue: Difficulty tracking design versions and changes.

Solution:

- Use Version History: Utilize Figma's version history to track changes and revert to previous versions.
- Naming Conventions: Adopt consistent naming conventions for files and components.
- External Tools: Integrate with version control systems like GitHub or use Figma plugins for better version management.

Accessibility Issues

Issue: Designs do not meet accessibility standards.

Solution:

- Accessibility Plugins: Use plugins like Stark to check color contrast, simulate color blindness, and ensure accessibility.
- Design Tokens: Implement design tokens to maintain consistent use of accessible colors and fonts.
- Inclusive Design: Follow best practices for inclusive design, such as providing alt text for images and ensuring keyboard navigability.

File Organization Problems:

Issue: Difficulty managing and navigating through large or complex design files.

Solution:

- Layer Naming: Use clear and descriptive names for layers and groups.
- Organize Frames: Group related elements into frames and sections.
- Libraries: Utilize Figma libraries to keep components, styles, and assets organized and easily accessible.

By addressing these common issues with practical solutions, you can ensure a smoother and more efficient workflow in Figma, enhancing both your productivity and the quality of your design work.

12.1 Resources

Here are some resources to help you learn more about Figma and its functionalities:

Official Figma Resources:

- Figma Help Center: https://help.figma.com/hc/en-us/categories/360002051613-Get-started
- Figma Design System Resources: https://help.figma.com/hc/en-us
- Figma Blog: https://www.figma.com/blog/
- Figma YouTube Channel: https://www.youtube.com/channel/UCQsVmhSa4X-G3lHlUtejzLA

Community-Driven Resources:

- Figma Resources: https://figmaresource.com/
- UI Hut (Figma Plugin Community): https://uihut.com/
- UX Planet (Figma Articles): https://www.figma.com/community/file/1116222343113939545/ux-planet

Social Media:

- Follow Figma on Twitter: https://twitter.com/figma

- Join the Figma Community on Facebook: https://www.figma.com/community/file/1134525529311722760/facebook-design (Search for Figma Community groups)

Learning Platforms:

- Become a Figma Masterclass: https://www.skillshare.com/en/browse/figma (Skillshare offers various Figma courses)

- LinkedIn Learning: https://www.linkedin.com/learning/ (Search for Figma courses)

- Udemy: https://www.udemy.com/course/learn-figma/ (Search for Figma courses)

These resources offer a wide range of information on Figma, from beginner tutorials to advanced techniques and design system management tips. You'll also find a vibrant online community where you can connect with other designers, ask questions, and share your work.

CHAPTER THIRTEEN
APPENDIX

Glossary of Figma Terms

Artboard:

- A design canvas where elements are created and arranged, also known as a "frame" in Figma.

Auto Layout:

- A feature that automatically arranges and resizes elements within a frame based on specified rules, enabling responsive design.

Boolean Operations:

- Tools for combining shapes in various ways, such as union, subtract, intersect, and exclude, to form complex shapes.

Component:

- A reusable design element that can be used across multiple frames and projects. Updates to the main component reflect in all instances.

Constraints:

- Rules that dictate how an element resizes or repositions when its parent frame is resized.

Design System:

A collection of reusable components, styles, and guidelines that ensure design consistency across a project.

Frame:

- A container for design elements, similar to an artboard. Frames can be nested within other frames.

Instance:

- A copy of a component that inherits properties from the main component but can be customized independently.

Library:

- A collection of components, styles, and assets that can be shared and reused across different projects.

Overlays:

- Interactive elements that appear on top of the current screen, often used for pop-ups, modals, or tooltips in prototypes.

Plugin:

- Third-party tools that extend Figma's functionality, offering additional features and integrations.

Prototype:

- An interactive mockup that simulates the user experience of a design, used for testing and validation.

Styles:

- Predefined sets of properties like colors, typography, and effects that can be applied to elements for consistency.

Variants:

- Different states or versions of a component managed within a single main component, useful for components with multiple configurations.

Vector Networks:

- A drawing method allowing for flexible and complex vector shapes, enabling connections between multiple points.

Version History:

- A feature that tracks changes made to a design file, allowing users to review and revert to previous versions.

View Only:

- A permission setting that allows users to view a design file without making any changes.

Anchors:
- Points in a vector shape that define its path's curvature and angles, altering the shape when moved.

Arc Tool:
- A tool for creating circular and semi-circular shapes with adjustable radii and angles.

Asset Panel:
- A panel for managing and accessing components, styles, and other reusable design elements in your projects.

Breadcrumbs:
- A navigation tool that shows the hierarchy of frames, groups, and layers you are working within.

Comments:
- Notes and feedback added directly to a design file for collaboration and communication among team members.

Cursor Chat:
- A feature showing collaborators' cursors in real-time for interactive and synchronized teamwork.

Device Frame:
- A visual representation of a device added to a frame to simulate how a design will look on that device.

Drafts:
- A personal workspace for creating and storing design files before moving them to team projects.

Grid Styles:
- Predefined grid settings applied to frames to help align and structure designs consistently.

Interactive Components:
- Components with built-in interactions and states, such as hover and click, to create dynamic prototypes.

Jumps:
- Links in prototypes that connect elements to different frames or overlays, simulating user navigation.

Layout Grids:
- Grids applied to frames to maintain consistent spacing, alignment, and proportions throughout designs.

Masks:
- Shapes used to hide or reveal parts of other layers, useful for custom cropping and clipping effects.

Multi-player:
- Figma's real-time collaboration feature allowing multiple users to work on the same design file simultaneously.

Nudge Amount:
- The distance an element moves when using arrow keys for precise positioning, which can be customized.

Presentation Mode:
- A view mode displaying the design in full-screen, ideal for presenting prototypes and design concepts.

Project:
- A collection of related design files and resources organized within a team or personal workspace.

Sections:
- Dividers added to a frame to organize and group content, useful for creating structured layouts.

Styles Panel:

- A panel for creating, managing, and applying text, color, and effect styles to ensure consistency in designs.

Team Library:

- A shared repository within a team for storing and accessing components, styles, and assets.

Text Box:

- A container for text that allows for adjustments in width, height, and alignment, used for adding and formatting text

Widget:

- Interactive elements added to Figma files to extend functionality, similar to plugins but embedded within the design.

Zoom:

- The ability to magnify or reduce the canvas view to focus on details or see the entire design layout.

Understanding these terms will enhance your proficiency with Figma, allowing you to navigate and utilize the platform more effectively.

THANK YOU FOR READING

Printed in Great Britain
by Amazon